AVIATION IN SCHOOL
AND COMMUNITY

COMMITTEE ON AVIATION EDUCATION

Appointed by the American Council on Education

HARRY BARD, *Chairman*
Assistant Director, Curriculum Bureau, Department of Education, Baltimore, Maryland

HAROLD E. MEHRENS, *Secretary*
Deputy Director, Aviation Education Staff, Office of Program Coordination, Civil Aeronautics Administration, Washington, D.C.

WILLIS C. BROWN
Specialist for Aviation Education, U.S. Office of Education, Washington, D.C.

GEORGE DENEMARK
Executive Secretary, Association for Supervision and Curriculum Development, National Education Association, Washington, D.C.

ROBERT W. EAVES
Executive Secretary, Department of Elementary School Principals, National Education Association, Washington, D.C.

PAUL E. ELICKER
Executive Secretary, National Association of Secondary-School Principals, National Education Association, Washington, D.C.

EARLE T. HAWKINS
President, Maryland State Teachers College, Towson, Maryland

J. GORDON HIGGINS
Assistant Supervisor, Secondary Education, Virginia State Board of Education, Richmond, Virginia

EBER W. JEFFERY
Department of History, Public Schools, Washington, D.C.

THEODORE P. WRIGHT
Acting President and Vice-President for Research, Cornell University, Ithaca, New York

Toward a better understanding of child growth and development; and the recognition of interest, purpose, and experience as important factors in learning (Trend 1). A sixth-grade unit recording "Famous First Flights."

Aviation in School and Community

H. E. MEHRENS
Editor

AMERICAN COUNCIL ON EDUCATION
IN COOPERATION WITH
CIVIL AERONAUTICS ADMINISTRATION

PRINTED IN THE UNITED STATES OF AMERICA BY
JUDD & DETWEILER, INC., WASHINGTON, D.C.

THE PROJECT CONTRIBUTORS

Director: HAROLD E. MEHRENS

Group Leaders: WALTER S. ASLING, ARTHUR GRIFFIN,
WILHELMINA HILL, CHAPIN R. LEINBACH,
HARRY G. ZARITSKY

MEMBERS OF THE 1952 AND 1953 INSTITUTES
FOR AVIATION EDUCATION LEADERSHIP

California: ROBERT T. BRUNNER, Burbank; CHARLES CRECELIUS, Torrance; PAUL F. DEVINE, Los Angeles; THOMAS L. NELSON, Berkeley; MRS. THOMAS L. NELSON, Berkeley; W. EARL SAMS, Sacramento; J. DOUGLAS WILSON, South Pasadena

Colorado: WELLINGTON M. LEWIS, Denver; LUKE G. TERRY, Denver

Connecticut: CHARLES H. ABELL, New Haven; ANTHONY W. BARCEWICZ, East Hartford; CHARLES H. KAMAN, Simsbury; CHARLES KIRCHNER, Newington; STANLEY H. LORENZEN, Manchester

Delaware: THOMAS W. HOWIE, Wilmington

District of Columbia (Washington): EVELYN CAMPBELL, GLADYS M. CHAPPELLE; L. ARNOLD ENGEL; MYRTLE A. FENTRESS; CARL F. HANSEN; KEITH C. JOHNSON; WILLIAM McROBERTS; DON RYAN MOCKLER; A. C. NORTHROP; RALPH B. TIGNOR

Florida: ROBERT D. DOLLEY, Coral Gables; THEODORE A. KOSCHLER, Miami

Georgia: E. B. BROWN, Atlanta; VICTOR B. HANSARD, Alpharetta

Hawaii: LOTTIE CANADY, Honolulu

Illinois: PAUL B. HALE, Urbana; ERIC H. JOHNSON, Urbana; GEORGE E. JONES, Park Ridge; ARTHUR J. LA POINTE, Chicago; MARY G. LUSSON, Chicago; ANTHONY MARINACCIO, Peoria; MELVIN R. MATTHEW, Decatur

Indiana: ERNEST R. THIEL, Indianapolis

Kansas: ELLSWORTH GREEN, JR., Kansas City

Kentucky: VERNON BINGHAM, Frankfort

Louisiana: WILLIAM K. BOHNSTORFF, New Orleans; EDWIN W. ELEY, New Orleans

Maryland: RALPH ANGEL, Hyattsville; FRANK B. BROOKS, JR., Bethesda; S. E. EMMONS, JR., Baltimore; G. JAMES GHOLSON, Hyattsville; JEAN McGREGOR, Silver Spring; JAMES M. SKIDMORE, Laurel; DONALD D. WEBSTER, Bethesda

Massachusetts: BROTHER MARINUS, Boston

Michigan: ROBERT E. LE ANDERSON, Detroit; STEPHEN A. PARTINGTON, Lansing; ELMER F. PFLIEGER, Pleasant Ridge; GERALD E. WHITE, Pontiac

Minnesota: ROWLAND C. ANDERSON, St. Cloud; J. ALBERT OSTER, St. Paul; E. DUDLEY PARSONS, JR., Minneapolis; WALTER J. ROCK, St. Paul

Missouri: LEE LAMAR, Jefferson City; J. GLENN TRAVIS, Independence

Montana: MAC JOHNSON, Cut Bank

New Jersey: CATHERINE BLEWITT, Newark; LEHMAN C. SHUGART, Elizabeth; WILLIAM R. SMITH, Newark

New Mexico: LESTER HITCHENS, Albuquerque

New York: ANN BROWN, Bronx; FLORENCE BRUMMER, Brooklyn; F. HERRICK CONNERS, Cohoes; WILLIAM B. KAMPRATH, Buffalo; GERRY LEIGHBODY, Buffalo; EUGENIE G. NADELMAN, Richmond Hill; DOROTHY W. ROSWICK, Forest Hills; FRANK WOEHR, Harrison

Ohio: BENJAMIN F. FRANKLIN, Cleveland; STERLING J. ORCHARD, Cleveland

Oklahoma: TED ANDERSON, Tulsa; MARSHALL LAKIN, Stillwater; S. ARCH THOMPSON, McAlester

Pennsylvania: H. EDWARD BRUNN, Nanticoke; GEORGE W. WILSON, Scranton

South Carolina: GEORGE W. HOPKINS, Columbia; PEARLE ROBINSON, Columbia; CHRISTINE SMITH, Entawville; S. DAVID STONEY, Columbia

South Dakota: M. L. REYNOLDS, Pierre

Texas: ROGERS BARTON, Austin; JESS CARDWELL, Dallas; CLIFF B. GREEN, Austin; DONALD JACKSON, Austin

Utah: MARK LLOYD, Salt Lake City

Vermont: GILBERT W. CALKINS, Northfield

Virginia: J. GORDON HIGGINS, Richmond; HOMER D. HUMPHREYS, West Point; JOSEPH A. PICKARD, Lynchburg

Washington: ERNEST W. CAMPBELL, Seattle; LYLE STEWART, Seattle

Wisconsin: B. C. KORN, Milwaukee

CONTRIBUTORS TO CHAPTERS 6 AND 7

Members of the Committee on Aviation Education, appointed by the American Association of School Administrators

HERBERT BRUNER, *Chairman,* Superintendent of Schools, Minneapolis, Minnesota; EVAN EVANS, Superintendent of Schools, Winfield, Kansas; DONALD MARSHALL, Assistant Superintendent of Schools, New Orleans, Louisiana; JOHN W. PARK, Superintendent of Schools, Albany, New York; DON R. SHELDON, Superintendent of Schools, Prescott, Arizona; DONALD E. TOPE, Superintendent of Schools, Phoenix, Arizona; FREDERICK B. TUTTLE, Superintendent of Schools, Westerly, Rhode Island.

Preface

THIS HANDBOOK WAS prepared by supervisors of instructional programs who became interested in enriching their programs by drawing information from areas of human activity outside the schoolroom. It is intended for the use of all leaders in education whose educational viewpoint impels them to follow well-defined curricular trends. The content treated relates to aviation and the peculiar and significant implications of human flight, be these political, social, economic, or military. The handbook also concerns itself with the application of general, forward-looking educational techniques to a single curricular problem area. However, the techniques it considers may be employed not only with aviation information, but also in terms of any information pertinent to general education and student development.

The book attempts a number of tasks. It reveals a need for contemporary concern with aviation as a factor in the destiny of humanity. It attempts to outline the responsibilities placed upon education as a result of the advent of aviation, and it offers aid to the supervisor who would guide his teachers to discover informational sources and employ proper educational procedures to meet these responsibilities.

It also draws upon current aviation education practices of representative school systems throughout the United States and demonstrates how such practices support the trends in curriculum improvement which herald the advent of a truly democratic approach to education.

HARRY BARD, *Chairman*
Committee on Aviation Education

Acknowledgments

IN THE PREPARATION OF this book, the Civil Aeronautics Administration has gladly cooperated with many individuals and groups who joined efforts in an attempt to help educational interests find satisfactory ways to solve the educational problems generated by the advent of human flight.

Without the fine cooperation and service of the members of the 1952 and 1953 Aviation Orientation Institutes, and of their group leaders, whose names appear on pages v and vi, this book could not have been produced. Scholarship donations made by industry members of the Air Transport Association and the Aircraft Industries Association enabled the attendance of many of the conferees. Among those contributing were the following: American Airlines, Inc.; Bell Aircraft Corporation; Boeing Airplane Company; Continental Air Lines, Inc.; Delta, Chicago, and Southern Airlines, Inc.; Eastern Airlines, Inc.; Hughes Aircraft Company; Lockheed Aircraft Corporation; National Airlines, Inc.; North American Aviation, Inc.; Northeast Airlines, Inc.; Northwest Airlines, Inc.; Pan American World Airways, Inc.; Trans World Airlines, Inc.; United Air Lines, Inc.; United Aircraft Corporation.

Other scholarship contributions were made by the New York Port Authority and the State Departments of Aeronautics of Kansas, Missouri, Oklahoma, South Carolina, and Texas.

Representative chamber of commerce groups throughout the United States took a positive interest in the conferences and Chamber of Commerce members from Washington, D.C.; Baltimore, Maryland; Los Angeles, California; Scranton, Pennsylvania; and Cleveland, Ohio, were numbered among the contributors.

The help made available to the project by the advisory committees of the American Council on Education and of the American Association of School Administrators was of great value and was sincerely appreciated.

The Civil Aeronautics Administration also wishes to acknowledge the whole-hearted assistance given the Aviation Orientation Institute by the U.S. Department of Defense, the U.S. Office of Education, and the Civil Air Patrol. Not only did these agencies provide challenging firsthand aviation experience or other educational experiences for institute members, but they also loaned the services of their personnel to the success of the project.

A most important contribution to orientation was the lectures provided by the Air Transport Association of America, the Aircraft Industries Association, the military services, the Office of Education, the Civil Air Patrol, the Conference of Aviation Organizations, the Civil Aeronautics Board, and the Civil Aeronautics Administration.

I also want to acknowledge the sympathetic support given to the project by my colleagues Mr. Wiley R. Wright, chief of the General Aviation Staff, and Mr. J. D. Blatt, Assistant Administrator for Program Coordination.

It is the sincere belief of the Aviation Education Staff of the Civil Aeronautics Administration that educational leadership will continue to draw upon the resources of all interested in aviation and its implications whenever such services can contribute to the purposes of education.

H. W. SINCLAIR, *Chief*
Aviation Education Staff
Civil Aeronautics Administration

Contents

1. The Aviation Education Movement

IN 1903 OCTAVE CHANUTE, one of the nation's foremost pioneers in aeronautical engineering, in commending the Wright brothers following the historic flight at Kitty Hawk, had this to say: ". . . Its [the heavier-than-air craft] first application will probably be military. . . . The machine will eventually be fast; they [aircraft] will be used in sport; *but they are not to be thought of as commercial carriers.*"[1]
The draperies that hide the future from the present opened for Chanute sufficiently to allow him only the briefest of glances. He predicted accurately in the first three statements above quoted. That he failed to comprehend, in 1903, the tremendous role the aircraft has come to play in the world of affairs can be illustrated by any schoolboy conversant with the hundreds of tasks performed each day by the airplane in its routine activities.

Only thirty years after Octave Chanute made his 1903 pronouncement, the aircraft made possible negotiations between American petroleum experts and Ibn Saud, late King of Saudi Arabia, which not only won the Arabian American Oil Company the right to develop one of the richest oil reserves of the world, but also brought in its wake a train of events which forcefully demonstrate the airplane's social significance.

Saudi Arabia, because of the use of aircraft in commerce, was confronted with the problem of transforming itself from a feudal into a modern society without taking any of the intervening steps granted other social systems. Space

[1] Smithsonian Institution Annual Report for 1903.

1

allows only a general reference to Saudi Arabia's problems and to the aviation events which brought them about. It permits us only to observe that the oil interests there have been quick to educate the Arabs to an understanding of the aviation age and to perform the skills required of those employed in aviation.

Saudi Arabia is not an isolated case. Aviation's impact is felt in every corner of the world. Complex societies feel this impact much more keenly than do the more primitive nations. It is not surprising, then, that a group of forward-looking educators have seized upon aviation to symbolize the tempo of modern life. No other recent technological development in terms of its over-all impact can so well point up the dangers resulting from failure to make appropriate social application of and adjustments to the discoveries of science and the inventions that follow.

The Problem of Aviation Education

The content of aviation education prior to 1942 was defined generally in terms of aeronautical skills. However, the booklet *Air Conditioning Young America,* prepared jointly by the U.S. Office of Education and the Civil Aeronautics Administration, regarded the problem of aviation education as twofold, incorporating both skills in aviation *per se* and understandings of aviation's uses. At present the concept of aviation education can scarcely be distinguished from that of education in an aviation age, except that the former regards aviation as foremost among those influences which affect contemporary life. The problem of aviation education now is defined in terms of preparing an individual citizen to cope successfully with the circumstances of the aviation age.

If organized education accepts as an objective the guidance of youth and adults essential in terms of problems of an aviation age, then the additional tasks which fall upon the schools require that educational leadership become increasingly concerned with the employment of an educational method which will attain this objective. It has been said that a half-century must elapse before a new idea in education is accepted. This statement is perhaps true when a new idea is left to depend upon the vagaries of chance. If we must wait fifty years to employ a solution to the problem of education in an aviation age—aggravated by the technological advance of atomic research—human life may well disappear from this planet. The alternative is effective educational leadership.

An educational program designed to induct youth into the realities of life must employ whenever possible the direct-experience technique. This technique requires the educational use of all available community resources and facilities. Before industry-education cooperation becomes a reality, school and community should reach a higher degree of harmony of understanding than that which at the present time generally prevails.

The aviation education movement is important to both school and public. Educational leaders have long been sensitive to the problem posed by the cultural lag. They recognize that a function of the school is to narrow as much as possible the gap between the realities of the contemporary world and the comprehension, by both youth and adults, of the meaning of these realities. In the aviation age when technological achievement crowds upon technological achievement, and the tempo of life has correspondingly accelerated, the tendency is for the cultural gap to widen. One way to prevent this so-called cultural lag is to gear the school's general education program to current affairs. Hence, the importance of the aviation education movement which does just that.

Aviation touches all significant areas of contemporary life, and the teacher whose group undertakes an aviation project can guide his students so that his curricular activities neglect no area of essential understanding. It is an educational truism that a child is chiefly interested in those phenomena he observes in his surroundings. A well-established educational principle states that interest is essential to learning. The fact that the airplane is a familiar aspect of the environment of contemporary youth does not lessen his curiosity toward and interest in the aircraft and the part it plays in the drama of his day. Rather, it enhances this interest.

The teacher who fails to capitalize upon such a ready-made interest overlooks an opportunity. It is by subordinating the educational objectives which the teacher holds in mind to the need of his pupils to understand the tangible in their environment, that both teacher and pupil purposes are achieved.

To enrich any given course through the use of appropriate, up-to-date information serves to enliven a classroom activity. That aviation education succeeds in doing this is further evidence of its importance. The reader will immediately observe the relationship between such course enrichment and the problem of the "cultural lag." Much "slack" is taken up when class and teacher, rather than awaiting interpretation by a textbook author, undertake to discover for themselves the implication of yesterday's event for the subject of their study.

Such an undertaking, however, requires full use of all school and community resources. To place the administration and operation of the schools in the hands of trained experts does not imply that cooperating interests of a community have nothing to offer. The method of aviation education enlists the appropriate aid of the aviation facilities of a community. Little more than this need be done to convince the aviation industry of its stake in education.

Technological Aspects of Aviation Education

The one who views for the first time the installations and equipment of an aircraft factory is likely to be impressed by their complexities. At that instant he begins to develop a healthy respect for aviation. Bundles of electronic wires as large as the arm, millions of rivets in one aircraft structure, and vertical stabilizers as high as a five-story building, are but a few of the items involved in the aviation industry.

One who observes an airplane factory or airport operations learns respect for those who conceive, design, construct, install, maintain, and operate such highly technical facilities. The radar screen, which enables the controller in the tower to help orient pilots during low visibility weather conditions; approach systems which permit perfect landings when cloud ceilings are very low—these and many other devices bear witness that the aviation age is characterized by technological achievement.

Among those employed in centers of aviation activity are people such as the "aircraft-loftsman," the "project engineer," the "electronics engineer," the "air-frame assembler," the "armament technician." The occupations of these men and women are strictly characteristic of the aviation age. Many related occupations which have grown out of the development of the aviation age are very significant. In a comparatively short span of fifty years, aviation vocations and related occupations have completely changed the nature of many communities. People are confused by the rapid technological development of aviation—the understanding of which has been largely ignored in preparing youth for contemporary life. Educational leadership, to remedy this situation, should employ both immediate and long-range effort.

What modern youth must know about aircraft

From the viewpoint of the adult concerned with social progress and national welfare, it is important that modern youth recognize the fundamental social, economic, and political principles of the society in which he lives. From the adult viewpoint, it is also important that youth reach a general understanding of the scientific and technological principles underlying contemporary social changes.

From the youth's point of view, it is important only that he be given correct answers to his questions about aircraft (or whatever other tangible his teacher employs), as the authors of the *Aviation Education Source Book*[2] discovered. The nature of the questions he asks about aviation depends upon the stage of the youth's development. A preschool child may ask, "Do airplanes land on clouds?" The first-grader, "What makes the propellers go round?" As the maturity of the child increases, his interest broadens until from a detailed interest in the aircraft itself, his questions indicate an interest in all of its uses and in its future development.

Modern youth should have a fairly broad and general concept of aviation. Every boy and girl should know when aviation made its first appearance. Each should know how aviation grew into its present position of importance. Each should become aware of probable future developments in the field. This knowledge need not be detailed and extensive, but youth's understandings of aviation should be broad enough to make him appreciative of the tremendous impact of aviation on his way of life.

Youth should have a general understanding of the aircraft itself. It is desirable that all youth know in general about different types of aircraft, and about the work done by each different type. He should also know the scientific principles that make flight possible. He should know about the more conspicuous parts of an aircraft and how each operates. In a general way he should understand how aircraft are built and maintained.

Every youth of high school age should have a general concept of the following in their relation to aviation: map-

---

[2] Paul R. Hanna, *et al.*, *Aviation Education Source Book* (New York: Hastings House, 1946), pp. 819 ff.

reading, navigation, instruments, both navigational and engine, meteorology, and the governmental regulations pertaining to airmen, aircraft, airways, and airports. He should understand that aircraft have certain physical limitations, and that they need regular inspection for safety's sake. Finally, he should have some understanding of the organization of military and civil aviation—how vast in scope and significant each is and how complex is each in its operation.

Specialized aviation courses

A specialized course in aviation is one which treats the technological characteristics of aircraft. It is an elective course and meets the needs of a particular group of students. It is distinct from the general course in aviation understanding, which in a few high schools is offered to all students. The specialized aviation course is for those students who desire a more thorough and extensive study, presumably as preparation for later jobs. It is built around the theme of aviation rather than being correlated with some other school subject. Three such courses are thought to be advisable to meet the needs of the aviation industry, military aviation, and the aviation transport industry: a basic course, a shop course, and a flight course.

1. *Basic course.*—This course is broad and general in its nature so as to give a complete overview of aviation. It may be thought of as a prerequisite for further study and particularly as providing a basic foundation for the better understanding of the "aviation-skills" courses. In content it should cover the following aspects of aviation:
a) The effect of aviation on our living; its history, its tremendous growth and probable effect on the future.
b) The airplane: its parts, structure, types (including the helicopter and autogyro).
c) Theory of flight: air foil studies, forces acting on a plane, axes of rotation, stability, safety measures in flying.

d) Power plants and their components; all types of engines, including jets and gas turbines; propellers; carburetion; ignition; lubrication; fuels.

e) Flight instruments and their use.

f) Weather and the atmosphere: clouds, circulation of the air, winds, storms, weather maps, fronts, forecasts, flight advisory service.

g) Aerial navigation: latitude and longitude, aeronautical charts, the magnetic compass, dead reckoning, celestial navigation, radio navigation, radar navigation.

h) Air traffic control: the Civil Aeronautics Administration; Civil Aeronautics Board regulations; at airports; along airways.

i) National and international problems of control.

j) Airports: classes, runways, airport lighting, administration buildings and terminals, hangars and service facilities, refueling facilities, fire and crash emergency equipment. Federal aid to airports program.

k) Vocational opportunities in aviation.

Since this course is more or less technical, it should require special teacher qualifications. It should meet five days a week during the school year and be offered in the upper years of the senior high school. Credit should be given toward graduation.

2. *Shop course.*—Aviation has need for mechanics in the manufacture and maintenance of airplanes. Many youths have a desire to do this type of work. As preparatory toward their further education in this field, it is recommended that the high school offer a one-year shop course in aviation in the industrial arts sequence of technical courses. The teacher must have special qualifications. The course should be offered to seniors, and one year of credit should be given toward graduation. It would prepare the student to undertake the

further study necessary to qualify him for the appropriate technical ratings and subsequent employment in aviation.

3. *Flight course.*—To meet a serious need for pilots, both in commercial and military flying, it is recommended that in the senior year a one-semester flight course be given with a maximum of fifteen hours of actual flight training and a minimum of eight hours of dual flight. Students enrolling in this course must be sixteen years of age and must have completed the one-year basic course. It will require a teacher with a flight instructor rating; hence, the cooperation and services of a local flight operator. It is suggested the instruction begin with students in the first semester of the twelfth year, so that if the required hours of flight cannot be acquired in one semester they may be completed in the second semester. One semester of credit should be given toward graduation. The suggested flight course does not offer the complete instruction necessary to obtain a private pilot rating. The additional instruction must be obtained from the local flight operator or a Civil Aeronautics certificated flight school.

SOCIOLOGICAL CHARACTERISTICS OF THE AVIATION AGE

The very fact that the speed of air transportation has drawn world centers closer together has many sociological implications. It has increased opportunity for interchange of ideas. As a result of our closer association with other peoples, American democratic concepts are receiving almost universal consideration; travel by air broadens education and provides new opportunity for people of other lands to view Americans in their true perspective.

The aviation age has truly been a predominant force in the removal of geographical barriers. One has only to recall the numerous achievements of the airplane in the last World War. Thousands of troops were moved by air. Long distances were covered in a very short time. Airplanes regularly flew all manner of equipment and supplies into hitherto inaccessible terrain. And the more recent Berlin airlift was an outstanding example of the effectiveness of the airplane in bridging political as well as geographic barriers in a difficult international situation.

To visit a port of entry for aircraft helps one to appreciate the significance aviation plays in eliminating geographic barriers. The airplane has brought about a situation of close human relations. It carries goods and peoples across national boundaries in a fraction of the time consumed by other transportation media. Its influences may create a better world understanding and cooperation, or they may aggravate international tensions. The aviation age brings with it a responsibility to us, the people of the United States, to present our culture in its most desirable aspects, if we are to succeed in spreading democratic ideas and practices.

The tendency toward defining distance in terms of air travel time should have changed our concept of geographic barriers. We should approach world problems with an air-age viewpoint. Oceans and polar icecaps no longer isolate us from the rest of the world. The world's problems are our problems.

Modern youth needs to know about aviation in terms of social change. Aviation has enabled nations to make rapid progress in the development of the potential economic and social aspects of their civilizations. This rapid progress, however, does not take place in all facets of a society at the same rate or at the same time. The resultant imbalances in the society are then manifested as social problems which come out of the lag existing between present practice and present need. Modern youth needs to develop an understanding both of present social problems that have been posed by an aviation age and of possible future problems that will emerge as new developments take place.

Of obvious importance is the role of the aircraft in transportation. Of equally obvious importance are the military uses of aircraft. Less well known are its industrial and agricultural uses. It is through the employment of information concerning current activities in all of these areas that the school's program may be enriched and that essential understandings may be brought to the nation's youth.

Youth needs to understand that social changes normally come about very slowly but that forces such as aviation have accelerated certain aspects of the total process. Such an understanding will emphasize the present and future need for attention to be given to the social problems thus created. In addition, youth must develop an understanding that we live in an interdependent world in which forces at work in other societies have direct and immediate influences upon our own society.

Modern youth needs to know about the economic aspects of aviation. A visit to a large airport will quickly convince any person that aviation has become one of our largest industries. The investment in planes, hangars, offices, and other facilities requires the employment of almost every skill known to modern business. In addition to the aviation business itself, the observer notes many related businesses, such as restaurants, drugstores, and bookstores operated at airports.

It is apparent that many persons possessing technological skills are required to operate the aviation industry. Designers, fabricators, pilots, and mechanics must build and operate planes. Many clerical workers and others possessing varied business skills are needed to carry on the business of aviation.

New marketing areas have been opened by air transportation. Areas far from production centers can be supplied with perishable goods, such as food and flowers. Isolated communities, inaccessible by other means of transportation, can be reached quickly by various types of aircraft. Medicines can be rushed to the sick when time is literally a matter of life or death. Supplies and personnel can be sent to devastated areas when natural disaster strikes.

Methods of business operation have been changed by the speed of air transportation. Many businesses have been able to reduce inventories, handle perishable items, keep abreast of new styles, and utilize inaccessible sources of materials because of the speed of aircraft. The businessman is able to reorganize all his efforts and make the most economical use of time. The aviation industry is best fitted to handle any product that demands speed in moving.

In the interest of conservation, national and state agencies use airplanes to reseed large forest areas. Burned-over forests and eroded areas are reseeded by airplane in one-fiftieth of the time required by any other method.

As it becomes necessary for our highly industrialized society to use more adequately our natural resources, the geographical survey is becoming more and more important. Aerial surveys bring knowledge of vast and hitherto inaccessible areas. Uranium and other critical minerals are now discovered by means of the versatile airplane. The airplane is gaining increased acceptance as a tool of industry. The so-called executive-type airplane is being used in many large industries. By the use of air transportation an executive can supervise a much wider area than surface travel allows. Key personnel are often moved by aircraft from one industrial site to another with great saving of both time and money.

We all remember tales of the fence rider of the Old West days. The modern counterpart of this rugged individual uses the small, light airplane. Many hundreds of thousands of air miles are spent inspecting power transmission lines, oil pipelines, and other remote industrial installations. The light airplane enables farmers and ranchers to reach distant points of their holdings and to attend to stock in places inaccessible by surface travel. Its use in crop dusting and spraying increases the productivity of the land. New uses for aircraft are found every day.

The financial structure of the aviation industry has implications for every young person. Historically, all methods of transportation have passed through periods during which they needed material aid from government agencies. The aviation industry is new, and has received various subsidies, such as aid in building airports and the like. The need for government aid should pass as the industry grows. Students should understand the significance of the changes in our national economic order which aviation has brought about.

How To Meet Industry's Demands for Aviation Personnel

Today approximately 700,000 people are employed in aviation occupations not including those in the armed forces. In 1951, domestic scheduled airline passenger miles slightly exceeded Pullman passenger miles on railroads in the United States. These two facts graphically illustrate the present size of the aviation industry and point toward expansion in the future.

Our air transport services are a billion dollar industry. They carry passengers, mail, and freight along our nation's airways. Air freight does not mean "emergency" freight, but that freight transported by air in terms of a carefully planned transportation program is found to be economically feasible.

Air transportation can bring financial returns to a community fortunate enough to have a large airport within its boundaries. Consider the case of Elizabeth, New Jersey, where 96 percent of the business firms requested the reopening of the Newark airport within a few months after local ordinances closed that port of entry.

Let it be clearly understood that in our economic picture of the aviation industry, we must not consider the scheduled airlines as being the sole source of advantage to the community. For the scheduled airlines own only 2,000 of the 56,000 planes in our country. Today many tasks essential to the nation's economy are being done by aircraft far faster and far more effectively than they could be done by other means.

The fact that the present demands for technically trained personnel in the field of aviation far exceed the supply poses a problem for educational leadership. It appears to be a problem which vocational education alone cannot solve. *General education must lay a groundwork of understanding and interest upon which specialized and vocational education can build.*

Aviation's increasing importance both as an occupational field and as a world force should ensure its prominence in the general education afforded all young people. Its impact as a world force is such that no realistic present-day program of education can fail to include aviation in the curriculum from kindergarten through secondary education. When pupils are thoroughly grounded in aviation's place in world affairs they will be much better prepared to enter technical training for particular aviation jobs. This technical training can be provided by private aviation schools, colleges, the industry itself, and to some degree by public and private secondary schools. *Pupils who show particular interest in aviation should have opportunities to pursue this interest.* It is the responsibility of the educational leadership in the community to provide these opportunities.

School administrators, supervisory and resource personnel, and teachers have a definite responsibility to see that materials descriptive of aviation occupations are placed in the hands of interested pupils. Materials are available from the sources listed in chapter v. Bibliographies and lists of aviation materials have been prepared, which will help the teacher and pupil to discover information about aviation jobs. Audio-visual aids such as films, filmstrips, recordings, posters, and diagrams are generally available.[3] It is well to

[3] See pp. 70–72.

remember that field trips to airports and airplane factories, lectures by aviation personnel from industry and from government agencies, and interviews with aviation employees, all serve the needs of the student having a dominant interest in aviation.

Local interest, financial resources, and the needs of the industry are leading factors in determining whether vocational courses should become a part of the curriculum of a particular school. Close liaison with the aircraft industry and governmental agencies is necessary to evaluate needs of the industry (including all segments of aircraft manufacture). There must be a constant re-evaluation of needs, based on current statistics and trends. Obvious limitations, financial and otherwise, prevent public and private secondary schools from offering technical training to all the people needed in aviation. However, *vocational training in the less technical aviation jobs should be a part of secondary education in communities where aviation employs a substantial number of people.* This is being done in some of the larger cities of the United States. Other communities should offer an elective course in principles of aviation where there is sufficient interest and qualified instructors are available.

RELATIONSHIP OF AVIATION EDUCATION TO PROBLEMS OF NATIONAL SECURITY AND WORLD LEADERSHIP

The development of aviation has posed many problems that might have been minimized or avoided if growth had been at a slower rate. Military activities have operated to accelerate developments in aviation and its effects on civilization. At the same time, however, aviation has furnished a means whereby social changes may be accelerated by providing for a rapid flow of ideas and persons within and among nations of the world. These advances in communication make possible a linking-together of cultures and an interchange of ideas that may be utilized as a major factor in building informed understandings and feelings of mutual well-being among societies. Modern youth needs to develop an understanding of the potentialities for social change which exist in such rapid communication. Youth must be brought to realize that these potentials exist and to understand their relationship to international problems.

We can recapture the position in world affairs which we enjoyed at the close of World War II only when our program of education develops us as a nation of people conditioned to the air as the English in the Elizabethan era were conditioned to the sea. Events of that war demonstrated clearly that aircraft has destroyed for us the very favorable geographic situation we had previously held. No longer can we rest in the assurance that oceans and wastelands provided us barriers against potential enemies. Now we must make the air our medium and strive not only to discourage aggression through the strength of our air power, but also to work toward abolishing war as an instrument of diplomacy.

Leaders and peoples of the free nations must continue with firm patience to discover peaceful means for solving international problems. However, it appears necessary at the same time to forge weapons for defense. In World Wars I and II there was time for mobilization. World War III, if it comes, will be swift and devastating. The enemy will strike at many places, not just at military, industrial, or transportation targets but at population centers as well. Obviously, our defense must exist in such evident strength as to deter the attack. Our best insurance for peace is international recognition of the fact that we have the power to strike back swiftly and with retaliatory effect.

Supremacy of air power is essential to national security, prestige, and world leadership. In an aviation age prevalent with atom bombs, guided missiles, radioactive dust, and bacteriological contamination, a command of the air is an essential of an adequate defense. America cannot relinquish her position as the international leader in air power. Even Britain, whose tradition rightly has placed first reliance on naval power, now has assigned priority to air power. In our own country early in 1948 the Congressional Aviation Policy Board stated that "Until men of all nations can meet in good will in the council chambers of the world, anything less than this complete supremacy in air power is self-deception." [4]

The schools can make an important contribution to the nation by emphasizing in terms of defense the value of air transportation, both civil and military, of planes and equipment, of production, and of the need for continuing research and development. Vocational programs will need to help train craftsmen for the highly intricate and specialized tasks involved in the fabrication and operation of modern aircraft. Yet, at the same time, schools must give even greater emphasis to teaching youth to study social and political issues, to sift facts, and to explore all sources of information before reaching conclusions. They must urge the paramount importance of democratic and spiritual values. International tensions have been intensified by the advent of aviation, and these tensions can be eased only by understanding the forces which are operating to create the tensions.

ADJUSTING THE SCHOOL'S PROGRAM TO THE AVIATION AGE

Aviation education should be developed in terms of youth needs and problems. If this is to be accomplished, it will be necessary to keep in mind the ability levels of youth in terms of what is now known about how children grow and learn. Education should recognize the fact that often in aviation education the youngsters may have greater knowl-

[4] Congressional Aviation Policy Board, Congress of the United States, *National Aviation Policy* (Washington: Government Printing Office, 1948), p. 3.

edge than the teacher of some particular phase of aviation. Teachers should capitalize upon this student interest and acquaintance with aviation by providing opportunities for experiences in the form of developmental tasks. Vitalization of the existing program will be gained if these experiences are provided, thus aiding general education in attaining its goals.

Good curriculum planning procedure will not forget participation by the public. The public can contribute ideas, personnel, and resources for enrichment of the program. The public should be kept informed of the schools' policies and practices so that there will be understanding of the schools' approach in meeting the needs of boys and girls. A well-informed public means greater support for the schools. In every undertaking for improving the schools' service to youth, there should be cooperative effort by all.

Aviation aids in teaching basic subjects. The increasing scope of human knowledge imposes a heavy load upon educational personnel in order to meet the demands for a full general education program. A vigorous and selective process needs to be continually employed in determining the program that is necessary for all youth. In addition to the significant part which aviation has played and continues to play in our technological progress, the inclusion of aviation education in traditional subject matter will provide a definite enrichment and motivation of the instructional activities. This applies not only to the regular offerings of mathematics, social studies, science, and language arts but also to extraclass activities. The interest of youth in aviation in its many aspects definitely has a place in the pupil-activities program. For those schools which have adopted the core, or the common learnings, approach to program development, there is great opportunity for the pupils and the teacher to follow through with experience activities of meaning to the boys and girls. This approach provides a method which perhaps best facilitates the use of community resources.

The supervisor is the key person in adjusting the school's program to the aviation age.   It appears sometimes quite difficult in educational practice to act upon conclusions of education's policy makers.   The factors which bring about this situation are too well known to merit detailed discussion at this time.   It suffices to observe that the prime factor in bringing educational practices into accord with the conditions of the times is the educational leader who works most closely with the teacher—call such a person supervisor, helping teacher, coordinator, counselor, or by some other term more acceptable in a given school situation.   It is this person who should, above others, recognize the task that the changing world conditions impose upon education, and it is he who must take the lead in an effort to find the way of adapting his school's program to this task.

Aviation's total educational impact imposes many responsibilities upon educational leadership as embodied in the supervisor of instruction.   However, three general areas of supervisory responsibility emerge as of greatest significance. The supervisor has a responsibility for guiding the teacher in an aviation-age program.   He must establish good working relationships with those segments of his community which are in a position to serve his school's program; he must make available to his teachers information concerning all the resources for aviation education which his community can make available.   One of his responsibilities which must not be overlooked relates to adult education in aviation throughout his community.   The remaining sections of this volume are devoted to more detailed consideration of those supervisory responsibilities and how they may be best met.

Summary

The aviation education movement takes cognizance of the fact that the invention of the aircraft and the subsequent use of aircraft in doing the work of the world have drastically affected the pattern of contemporary living. The aircraft has stepped up the tempo of modern life, widening still further the gap between the school and the society it serves.

An educational program to serve adequately the aviation age must concern itself with the *technological* and *sociological characteristics* of such an age. The aviation education movement undertakes to involve the community in programs of organized education. It is convinced that to do this establishes realistic and vitalized educational procedures in a community. The purposes of aviation education differ from those of other educational programs in that they give emphasis to an environment rapidly changing as a result of aviation's impact. Of particular importance in the aviation education movement is the implication of aviation for problems of America's position in world affairs.

Supervisory responsibilities in education imposed by aviation relate to all major educational areas, including educational and vocational guidance and adult education. All youth in schools should become generally informed about the nature of aircraft and the many services aviation performs. They should understand those social, economic, and international aspects of aviation which are affecting or may affect the course of their lives and the destiny of their nation. They must above all realize that aviation is accelerating change in societies the world over.

2. Guiding the Teacher in an Aviation Education Program

A FEW SCHOOL SYSTEMS have a full-time supervisor of aviation education. This is a practice whose merit other systems should appraise. This supervisor can devote full time to encouraging teachers in curricular fields to employ in their courses relevant aviation information. He can be especially helpful to his teachers in terms of aviation information and aviation resources. He will aid in arranging field trips and visits to aviation installations, in conducting teacher institutes, and in providing orientation flights for the community served by the school. As a specialist he may teach specialized courses in aviation for both secondary school students and adults in evening schools.

The involvement of the community in the problem of modernizing education extends beyond the use of a cooperating agency to further a school program. It should include contributions by educational leadership to extraschool adult groups, and may well extend to establishing programs of adult education within the structure of organized education.

Perhaps it is well to remind those who desire to help others bring about understandings of changing concepts and establish new patterns of human behavior, that they should give teachers and others a share in making plans and reaching decisions about the methods of reaching these objectives. This means that an educational supervisor should not attempt to impose his own convictions of aviation's social implications upon those he supervises. Rather, before attempting any change in his school's curriculum, he must look to the techniques of group dynamics and involve his people, as a group,

21

in solving the educational problems engendered by aviation.

The supervisor must use the democratic process. Much thought and effort has been spent by curriculum specialists in many state departments of education and municipal schools in the preparation of plans for introducing aviation into the programs of the school systems of the state or municipality.[1] To employ without question such suggested plans or programs is not sufficient to the task. Through appropriate conferences involving the teachers and moderated by the supervisor, such plans must be appraised and used as points of departure in preparing courses of action acceptable to those concerned.

The part played by the supervisor must be positive and courageous. For the supervisor to employ the techniques of group dynamics does not mean for him to relinquish his prerogatives; however, it does mean that he must be democratic rather than dictatorial in his approach to this most vital understanding.

Teachers as well as their students must be ready before they learn. The supervisor may well observe the principles of readiness as he approaches the task of helping his teachers to employ in their teaching, knowledge of the forces which impinge upon our lives and our society. We may deplore the fact that some of the social concepts of many teachers antedate the impacts of aviation. However, we cannot reorient the thinking of these teachers solely by telling them about our new social forces. They must undergo additional experiences through which they are actively identified with the effect of these forces. It is the task of the supervisor to provide his teachers with the opportunity for experiences which will bring about in them a readiness and willingness to adapt their classroom program to a changing world.

[1] U. S. Department of Commerce, C.A.A. Office of Aviation Development, *State Plans, Programs, and Publications in Aviation Education* (Washington: Civil Aeronautics Administration, 1950).

Those in a school system charged with supervisory responsibilities must make certain that the teachers comprehend fully the basis of the aviation education movement. A first step in the supervisor's procedure would be to employ all means at hand to help his teachers grasp the importance of aviation understandings as well as their effectiveness in motivating pupil activity. In addition to employing the techniques referred to above—democratic discussion and actual experiences—the supervisor has available an excellent instrument in the audio-visual kit, with its accompanying manual *Aviation Education.*[2]

In the face of a contemporary conviction on the part of many educators that a given purpose can be accomplished through a variety of methods, it will be unpopular to argue for the employment of one procedure above another. Consequently, the best effort of the supervisor, in this respect, can be made as moderator, while the teachers he supervises, through the process of group action, investigate, gather information, organize their thinking, reach conclusions, and eventually define for themselves a procedure which they find appropriate in terms of both student and teacher needs and purposes. The teachers will find in such supervisory technique a clue to the method most suitable for their use in their own classroom situations.

How To Help the Teacher Use Community Resources in Aviation

Any school program which involves use of community resources requires liaison effort.[3] Such effort must be threefold. First, the supervisor, or someone he delegates, must reach an understanding with the cooperating agency. Next,

[2] Harold E. Mehrens and Harry G. Zaritsky, *Aviation Education—An Approach to a Modern Curricular Problem* (Washington: American Council on Education, 1951).

[3] Chap. iv treats the problem of establishing working relationships with cooperating groups.

he should inform his teachers of the service such agency is prepared to offer. Finally, he should instruct his teachers in the approach to use in arranging with such agency for the use of its facilities.

Obviously, the principal contribution which can be made to the school by an industry, agency, or other organization is information—information pertinent to a task confronting the classroom group. Much of this information is available in printed materials; other means of obtaining and transmitting to students information involve personal visits of the class to aviation installations, airports, and industries, and talks by aviation authorities from industry and government when students are encouraged to ask questions.

Workshops bringing together all these resources have been enthusiastically attended by teachers in a number of communities. The supervisor should hold preliminary meetings with his teachers, first, to define student interest, and, second, to determine the resources available to promote that interest. It must be kept constantly in mind that the best criterion to employ in program-making or selecting course content is student interest and curiosity. That the child's question may be naïve, or his problem simple, does not change the instructional method one iota. Normal curiosity establishes the best learning situations. Having ascertained desirable content of a workshop type of meeting, the supervisor should take the responsibility for careful planning of a cooperative program. Nothing should be left to chance. Each person —teacher, student, and aviation resource person—should be informed precisely of his role in the program.

Teachers must be provided information regarding community resources. Supervisors should provide teachers under their direction with a file of available resources. Such a file should include not only the name and location of a potential contributor, but a brief and accurate description of the nature of the contribution. Each file card, if ap-

propriate, should also show hours for visitation, number of
students permitted in each visiting group, telephone number
of the industry contact, age or grade level most likely to
profit from the visitation, whether or not a guide is provided,
time required by industry group to arrange visitation program, an orientation flight, and the like.[4]

THE SUPERVISOR'S RELATION TO THE PROBLEMS OF AVIATION EDUCATION IN CURRICULUM-MAKING

There was a time when curriculum-making undertook to
prescribe not only what to teach but also when to teach it.
In accordance with the principles that governed curriculum-
planning under those circumstances, the first big curricular
problem would have been to select for the student the information he must use, and the second problem would have
been to decide for student and teacher the appropriate time
to expose the student to such information. As a matter of
fact, the point of view that would have dictated these problems should still be held when the supervisor deals with
specialized or vocational preparatory courses in aviation.

The specialized aviation course

The role of the supervisor in curriculum-making as this
pertains to special and vocational fields is determined by
the nature of the specialized interest or vocation in question.
As a matter of fact, the content of the specialized course is
pretty well defined by the textbooks adopted. The selection
of a specialized text for secondary school use should be based
upon an analysis of the needs of those undertaking a chosen
career. Obviously, since public school aviation courses are,
for the most part, preparatory rather than terminal, the
supervisor's principal task in terms of such special courses

---

[4] Descriptions of listings from which some file data may be obtained are
given on pp. 70–72.

is to help determine course content (that is, choose the texts), specify when the courses should be taught, define the methods of keeping these up-to-date, and employ all the techniques of enriching such courses that are revealed elsewhere in this book.

The administrative policy of a given school system determines whether or not such courses should be offered. If the nature of the community served by the school justifies adding aviation courses to the curriculum, a wise administrator takes steps to include such courses. There is ample evidence at present to demonstrate a need for a much broader course offering in the field of aviation at the public school level than presently exists. In any event, the curriculum supervisor, in aviation or elsewhere, can define only what he believes to be curriculum needs. He can recommend only the adoption of the policy that he helps outline.

The role of the curriculum-maker in general education

In general education it may appear that the supervisor plays a subordinate role; he certainly shares the stage with others, since teachers, youth, and sometimes parents play their several parts. Because child growth and development, rather than organized subject matter, define the objectives of general education, scope and sequence take on meanings in general education quite different from the connotations they hold for specialized education. However, as a matter of fact, the task of the supervisor in general education is no less important than heretofore; it is different.

The over-all purpose of general education is development, that is, an individual's growth in terms of understandings, skills, knowledge, and attitudes pertinent to the general pattern of living rather than to a vocational field. As a matter of fact the individual generates his own growth in these areas. The function of the teacher is to make certain that the activities engaged in are essential and relevant to the growth desired. The curricular function of the supervisor is to help define the very general framework within which is permitted great flexibility of classroom activities, and to make certain that instructional materials and aids are adequate.

There are different schools of thought as to how the teacher function just stated can be performed. Sometimes a curricular viewpoint will assign a specific subject to the general curricular areas—understandings, skills and attitudes. Although special curriculum areas should be classified in terms of subject matter, general curriculum areas must be defined in terms of the attributes of human growth and development. For example, the subject of arithmetic is employed in the development of an essential skill. The child or youth has available for his use a text prepared by one skilled in the organization of information about arithmetic, including statements of principles and their illustration. Or, in the subject of literature an anthology of the world's classics is employed in the hope that it will make possible vicarious experiences through which attitudes commensurate with human values will be forthcoming. Since this approach, hallowed by tradition, is highly regarded by many of the country's leading educators, it must be given fair appraisal by its critics. The proof of any method is determined by its success in terms of its objectives.

A curricular philosophy is emerging in this country which its proponents believe has great merit in that it provides the child with opportunity to think logically. Procedures based upon this educational viewpoint encourage the student to search for information relevant to an immediate problem defined by his own interests, and, hence, to discriminate between the significant and the trivial. Final steps of procedure employed by this point of view enable a student to reach conclusions based upon fact and authority, and to agree with others as to courses of action based upon such conclusions.

Those teachers who have been most successful in adapting their classroom programs to employ this educational approach, reveal that children's activities are best motivated by problems—albeit, simple ones—that they accept as their own. They point out that, in the terms of problems which relate to the need for understandings, children reason very well indeed, readily develop discriminating powers, and moreover, realize quickly the importance of essential skills, and participate in drill activities that otherwise would have proved tedious indeed. This is not the place to describe the dynamic approach to education. It is sufficient to observe that students involved in such a program, rather than committing to memory information organized for them, are motivated to use such organized information as sources of the materials to be employed in efforts of their own, organizing the information they have gathered and creating for themselves.

The Supervisor and the Teacher in an Aviation-Age Program

Before the supervisor can be of any help to the teacher in introducing aviation into the school program, he must have a broad knowledge of the educational implications of aviation. In terms of aviation, he should know something of community resources and community aviation personnel. He should be conversant with audio-visual and other aids in this field so that he can make definite and worth-while suggestions that contribute to a successful enterprise. Above all, he should be informed concerning the present status of the aviation education movement.

Information imparted by supervisors should always be reliable. There is nothing more frustrating to a well-meaning and eager teacher than to find that his first few attempts in reaching for help are futile. Many teachers who needed guidance badly, and who with the proper guidance might have done a commendable job, have lost enthusiasm for a project because they were referred to sources which they found unreliable.

Teachers like to observe actual practices. After viewing a demonstration, the usual reaction is, "I've read and I've listened, but now I know what you mean." It is quite important that the supervisor make use of demonstration technique. It can be employed by the supervisor so that it becomes part of an in-service program for all teachers: all areas of relationship between education and aviation would be explored, techniques explained and demonstrated, units planned, opportunities for cooperation of community and school surveyed, and materials collected and evaluated.

The supervisor who makes practical application of theory in an actual classroom situation is generally effective. He sets up a series of demonstrations; teachers actually observe appropriate aspects of aviation integrated with the normal classroom work. Such aviation materials might imply a change of geographical concepts; they might involve comparison of the time it takes to get places by land, sea, and air; they might deal with what makes an airplane fly; or why does an airplane make noise; or why should an airport be convenient to a center of population, or what community interest has been most greatly influenced by the airplane, or any one of the numerous aspects of aviation with which pupils are concerned.

The supervisor in meeting with teachers of all grades should help to develop understandings of knowledge and skills which may be developed at each grade level. The topic of weather, for instance, may be considered at the kindergarten level and through the grades to the sixth year, but in each instance the method of approach and the form of approach will be different, and at each progress level there should be a broadening of the concepts learned.

A welcome supervisor in any school is one who is able to sit down with a teacher and assist him in his preplanning and move on from that state to working with the class in pupil-teacher planning periods. Subsequent visits should enable the supervisor to keep informed of the progress of a unit, to see whether or not the initial plans were adequate, and to suggest necessary changes.

Opportunities should be arranged for teachers to visit classrooms in which sound aviation education programs are in progress. The classrooms of teachers conducting successful aviation education activities might be designated as "pilot" classes.

Since one of the facets of supervision is the ability to select and encourage teachers with special aptitudes and interests, the supervisor should undertake to discover teachers especially interested in aviation and encourage each of them to become a resource person for the school, district, or other area.

The supervisor has another important task in the in-service education of the teacher. Just as we say it is important in education for pupils to feel a "need" for certain information, it is also very vital that teachers feel a "need" to impart such information. Therefore, the supervisor must help the teacher to understand the implications of teaching. To help him with this task, he may wish to employ extraschool sources. Films and other items produced either by the Civil Aeronautics Administration, or the airlines, can be very helpful in stimulating interest. A good speaker can sometimes inspire the necessary enthusiasm and effort and impart sound information. Once the teacher has acquired sufficient understanding, she will begin to realize that aviation is not necessarily a subject in itself, but has its place in science, mathematics, social studies, creative writing, reading, music, dramatic play, and art.

The supervisor might possibly take the lead in setting up for his school district, or any other area of which he is in charge, a room or a place for the display of aviation-age materials. Here, among other items, could be displayed the latest in texts, free and inexpensive materials, visual and audio aids, magazines, successful pieces of work completed by other teachers, bulletin boards, materials constructed by children. The material displayed should be available for use. To facilitate such use, it should be classified according to its appropriateness for different grade levels or subject-matter fields. It should be available to students on a loan basis.

The supervisor should encourage the organizing of model-building clubs and hobby clubs, the appropriate uses of leisure time, and should give the necessary administrative attention to details involved in providing time for these clubs to function.

Although between the kindergarten and sixth year, there is little opportunity for specialized study, the supervisor might guide the teacher toward finding the children with special aviation aptitudes and interests, and provide the guidance necessary to see that these students make the most of available opportunities.

Since an informed community is necessary to the success of any school program, the supervisor might encourage the teacher to invite parent participation in some of the aviation activities of student groups. Parents can often make vital contributions to educational projects and to teachers' workshops and discussion groups. At the same time they can gain important information for themselves. Parents who acquire a better understanding of the work the teacher does help to assure the success of the school's program. Effort should be made to discover the names of parents employed in aviation industries who can help in school and community aviation effort.

We approach this section on secondary education with the idea that curriculum-planning is most effective when it involves people in all fields of the school programs at both the elementary and the secondary levels. Ideally, the development of an aviation education program should involve parents, children, teachers, supervisors, and administrators. Practically, in most cases, it will include only teachers and supervisors. This makes the supervisor a key person in the development of any aviation education program.

Variation among secondary school programs must be taken into consideration. Some schools have general education or core programs with one or more supervisors responsible for the total school program. Others are organized departmentally, with supervisors assigned responsibility for specific subject-matter areas. We will devote a number of paragraphs to ways in which supervisors in each of these situations can help teachers.

General education

Those who advocate a program of general education recognize the fact that within the broad framework of preplanned problem areas the resourceful teacher can introduce her pupils to many meaningful experiences. Aviation should present unlimited possibilities for the development of a general education program in the secondary school.

The supervisor can be of invaluable assistance in such an undertaking. The very nature of his job allows him broader contacts which, if shared with pupils and teachers, will serve to enrich the experiences of all concerned. He can help teachers of the core or general education course to orient their teaching to the air age; help them shape their teaching to pupils' needs in aviation education; and help them use an experience approach rather than the ororverbalized procedure too often employed in secondary school teaching.

The departmentalized approach

In a school or school system organized along departmental lines the supervisor of each special subject must be able to help the teachers in his department to do an effective job of aviation education. He must be well informed and have a broad perspective with reference to aviation education. He must have a fund of ideas about using aviation to enrich his special subject-matter field. Sometimes he may need to encourage his teachers to incorporate into their courses relevant and significant facts from the field of aviation.

All social studies teachers and supervisors know that aviation events have particular significance for their field of study. All of the concepts of world understanding and citizenship have been brought into sharper focus since the advent of aviation. Geography must now be interpreted in the light of geopolitics.

The study of mathematics and science affords wide possibilities for employing the data of aviation. The science of air navigation requires the application of mathematical skills. Many scientific principles can be best taught in terms of their application to aviation and its related fields.

Excepting the core course, offerings in English composition provide secondary education its best opportunity to do creative study in aviation. There are many interesting aviation and related topics to be used as theme topics. Aviation also contributes many new words to the language. The literature of aviation is rich in materials appropriate throughout the secondary school. Above all, aviation has implication for instructional methods in foreign languages. Students in an air age should learn not the grammar, but the use of language of other nations.

Vocational education courses offer opportunity for general as well as specialized study in aviation. Model building becomes of importance in manual training courses. Exploratory courses in aviation careers prove important in the curriculum of vocational education departments.

TECHNIQUES FOR ADAPTING CLASSROOM PROGRAMS TO AN AVIATION AGE

Teachers need the help of administrators, curriculum specialists, and/or supervisors to plan a curricular program which includes aviation. Space does not permit a detailed report of effective techniques employed to this purpose,[5] but the following paragraphs describe some techniques which have been used with success.

Expand aviation interests

A first step toward employing aviation interests in the classroom is to establish an aviation-age environment appropriate to the objectives of the unit or course being introduced. News stories, pictures of aircraft provided from current magazines, posted and replaced periodically by the committee of students to whom this task has been delegated, help establish such an environment.

A second step is to prepare the class for consideration of appropriate aviation problems through discussion of such questions as: (*a*) What makes a plane fly?, (*b*) How is a plane constructed?, (*c*) How much do planes of various kinds cost?, (*d*) What uses are made of planes at our local airport?, (*e*) How can I learn to fly and how much does it cost?, (*f*) What career opportunities are there in aviation?, (*g*) How can I discover the job in aviation for which I am best suited?, (*h*) What interests, skills, and attitudes should

[5] For additional information see Harold E. Mehrens, *Adventures in Aviation Education* (Washington: American Council on Education, 1951).

a person possess before embarking upon a training program to become an aircraft mechanic?, (*i*) Where can I get the necessary training to become an aeronautical engineer?, (*j*) What skills that I can learn in elementary and high school are required of an aeronautical engineer?, (*k*) What are the immediate and future prospects for employment in the aviation careers in which I am interested?, (*l*) How is the airport in one's own community found?, Who owns and maintains it?, (*m*) How should communities be planned so that maximum benefit from air transportation can be derived?, (*n*) What influence has aviation had on global geography?, (*o*) How has aviation influenced the political world scene?, (*p*) What social influences are exerted by aviation that are of importance to me?

Recognize individual differences
but encourage group cooperation

The teacher must help each pupil select a problem that is appropriate to his interests, abilities, and special needs. However, as individual members of the class discover that their interests are common with others, they should be encouraged to combine their efforts. To do this effectively requires that committees be organized and tasks defined before work is begun.

Visits to the local airport and the aircraft manufacturing plant should be planned by the teacher working with a committee of the classroom group. A committee should explore orientation flights. After a visit to an aviation installation or a group flight, classroom discussion centered around the experience should be encouraged and the observations of individuals should be reported.

The class periodically should evaluate the efforts of each committee in terms of criteria agreed upon by the entire class during planning sessions. The teacher periodically should assess the progress of each pupil in terms of his individual capacities, personal and class objectives, and success as a contributing member of the group.

SETTING UP A REPOSITORY OF INSTRUCTIONAL AIDS AND MATERIALS

One of the best things that a curriculum department can do to help the teachers it serves is to provide a curriculum laboratory of teaching aids. The best supervisor or the most willing teacher cannot do a really good job unless provision is made for the necessary instructional materials and for easy access to them.

A curriculum laboratory may include authentic, factual material that can be obtained in the form of government pamphlets, CAA publications, and materials published by state education departments and aeronautics commissions. It may include study outlines from other school systems as well as collections of teaching units descriptive of actual classroom experiences. It should provide lists of films, filmstrips, and other audio-visual aids. It will make available all the instructional aids in aviation that the school's budget will permit. In addition to a collection of professional material, the curriculum laboratory may well have available for teacher and student use the attractive and practical materials produced by the air transport, aircraft, and related industries. All the materials contained in the curriculum laboratory should have been screened to determine their educational value.

An aviation education center (library-laboratory) may be in a separate building and may contain a Link trainer and such airplane parts as fuselage, engine, and a wing. Collections of printed materials of all types, filmstrips, pictures, maps and globes, and pamphlets will add to the effectiveness of a repository of this kind.

A repository should be accessible to all who can profit by its use. The size of the school system will govern whether there will be one central laboratory or many units distributed throughout the school district. Sometimes a room in a school is converted into a laboratory.

Whatever the local arrangement may be, instructional aids and materials should be arranged, classified, and indexed in such a way that the aviation education center will be used by teachers and pupils as source material that will be helpful in planning and developing units of work and projects, and in contributing toward the enrichment of subject-matter areas. The successful use of any collection of instructional material requires that such a collection be periodically checked for accuracy and validity and that it be kept up to date.

SUMMARY

Supervisory guidance of teachers and instructors in an aviation program should employ logical and effective techniques. Since it is important that those who carry out a plan have a voice in its preparation, it appears imperative that the supervisor use the democratic action technique in conference situations.

The employment of such a dynamic process assures that a teacher will have had the benefit of group assistance in reaching conclusions as to the need for an aviation education program and in defining his purposes in an aviation education program. In-service programs for teachers when conducted in accordance with the principles of group dynamics not only bring understandings of the "why" of aviation education but also help with problems of what to teach in this area, when to teach it, and where to teach it.

Supervisory guidance undertakes to establish harmonious relationships with those community agencies in a position to assist the school's aviation education program. It also undertakes to help teachers use the contributions of such agencies to enrich their classroom programs. The supervisor assures himself that his teachers are skilled in the special techniques required by the teacher and students who make use of current events in their activities, and that teachers and pupils have easy access to the instructional materials, aids, and devices essential to the successful outcome of these activities.

3. Promoting Industry Cooperation
in Aviation Education

IT IS HIGHLY DESIRABLE that education and the aviation industry develop a mutual understanding of each other's program. From such understanding should grow a better realization of the problems involved in any cooperative educational effort. Only such understandings can define the common areas of interest where cooperative effort can be used to mutual advantage, and in the general public's interest. Only through a dynamic program of cooperation may education and aviation each expect to make its best contribution to the society both serve. Through this cooperative effort, aviation is provided the means to present schools with current, accurate information, the dissemination of which is essential to the nation's welfare and security. In turn, education is provided the means to vitalize its program through the proper use of such information. A by-product of this cooperation is a growing respect on the part of the aviation industry and of education for the program of the other.

It is the purpose of this section to offer some guidance to the educational supervisor concerned with the problem of establishing a harmonious working relationship between the school and those aviation industries or interests in a position to contribute to the educational program of the community. The supervisor's task then is to encourage the use of aviation information, inform teachers of the resources available, and describe how they may be obtained and used to the best advantage. Above all, the supervisor must help the school capitalize upon the willingness of aviation interests to cooperate in making the facilities of aviation available for educational purposes.

The progressive school supervisor, charged with a responsibility in aviation education, can secure the help of many agencies and their representatives: governmental offices—federal, state, and local; the military services; the industry itself which maintains educational advisers and many special services to schools; aviation organizations; other school systems; and even international bodies. Publications—aviation, educational, and general—are plentiful, authoritative, and interesting to all students.

Governmental agencies

In all communities today there is some form of aviation activity. Mail is carried, people and freight are transported by airplane, forests are protected, cattle are watched, crops are dusted. Such activities demand one degree or another of governmental interest and control. The governmental office most concerned with a given activity is always ready to make educational service available. The postmaster can tell about air mail, the Air Force recruiting officer about his branch of the service and what it offers youth, the forest service can relate dramatic tales about the smoke-jumper.

A first contact might well be the federal Civil Aeronautics Administration, the Civil Air Patrol, or the Air Force Association. A communication should be directed to the state department of education asking for the name of the official in charge of aviation education. In most states there are aviation commissions or bureaus whose duty it is to encourage and promote the welfare and development of aviation. In many cities there are airport commissions concerned with airport construction and operation. The names and addresses of representatives of the Civil Aeronautics Administration and of many other aviation officials and agencies may be found in the *American Aviation Directory.*[1]

In addition to the potential sources of educational assistance mentioned above, there are, at the federal government level, the Department of Agriculture, the Air Navigation Development Board, Aircraft Production Board, Coast and Geodetic Survey, the U.S. Coast Guard, the U.S. Weather Bureau; the Office of Education of the Department of Health, Education, and Welfare; Committee on International Airports, National Advisory Committee for Aeronautics, National Production Authority, Post Office Department, Search and Rescue Agency, Smithsonian Institution, and the State Department. Telephone directories and aviation directories will indicate the federal agencies which have branch offices in the community.

The military agency most greatly concerned with aviation is obviously the U.S. Air Force. From it can be secured speakers, educational films, literature, and demonstrations of aviation equipment. Upon proper request, class and teacher visits to military establishments can be arranged. The United States Navy offers materials and services comparable to those of the U.S.A.F. Also of importance as cooperating interests are the United States Army and the Marines. All of these services have their own aviation components which can render valuable support and liaison functions. A request to the Public Relations Office of any of the services will bring about courteous cooperation.

The aviation industry

The resources available to the school from the aviation and related industries are easily secured. Industry is concerned with public relations; it wants to promote public

[1] *American Aviation Directory* (Washington 5: American Aviation Publications, Inc.). Names and addresses of C.A.A. educational advisers will be sent on request to Civil Aeronautics Administration, Washington 25, D.C.

understanding. A company desires to encourage consumers to use its products. In order to recruit efficient workers, it seeks the understanding of its community. In general, industry agrees that the schools provide an excellent public relations medium. Industry recognizes its stake in education and desires an efficient school program.

It is the responsibility of school personnel to investigate the opportunities industry offers for cooperative service. Among such industrial concerns are included the scheduled air carriers, nonscheduled air carriers, air express and air freight companies, air-taxi operators, and other airport operators. The aircraft manufacturing industry, which should be numbered among the cooperating interests, will also prove a valuable source of assistance. Manufacturers of aircraft power plants and of aircraft and propellers are typical agencies. The fact that bauxite ore is mined to make aluminum, that cotton is grown to make airplane fabric, and that many raw materials go into the making of an airplane, an aviation engine, or an aviation instrument, will call to mind many industries in a position to contribute information concerning some aspect of aviation that touches American life.

Aviation organizations

The alert schoolman recognizes that there are many aviation organizations in a position to cooperate in the field of aviation education. Among these are clubs which represent persons engaged in fields such as model building, flying, gliding, rockets; also flying farmers, and "old timers." Preeminent among such organizations is the National Aeronautic Association.

In addition to the above, professional education associations should be used, both those with specific interests such as the National Aviation Education Council and the University Aviation Association, and others with more general interest in aviation education, such as the several departments of the National Education Association. The Boy Scouts, Girl Scouts, Wing Scouts, the Civil Air Patrol, all of these and many civic organizations should be explored by educational leadership in the interest of school and community cooperation in a program of aviation-age education.

Other school systems

An understanding source of help to a school supervisor in incorporating aviation in the school curriculum is other schoolmen. There are many schools which already have on-going programs of education in which aviation plays an important part. Teachers and supervisors experienced in aviation education can explain their programs and help others to move forward in this field. Certain high school supervisors, whose names can be secured through professional contacts, can explain their programs of aeronautics and their aviation mechanics courses. Institutions of higher learning doing work in aviation can be of help. All are eager to explain their programs to potential students. Some states —California and New York for example—offer aviation courses at the junior college level. Many engineering colleges offer courses in aeronautical engineering. In addition to these specialized courses at the post-high-school level, many teacher education institutions incorporating aviation in their program can provide information about the location of cooperating agencies and the assistance that is available.

International agencies

There are many international agencies which may be considered valuable resources in the field of aviation education. The work of the United Nations is closely dependent upon aviation. The *Federation Aeronautique Internationale* is one of those agencies rich in aviation background. The International Civil Aviation Organization should not be overlooked by education leaders as an important cooperating interest. Its headquarters are at Montreal, Province of Quebec, Canada.

Publications

There are a number of magazines devoted to aviation, and many professional journals and general magazines and books carry information about aviation matters and are suggestive of sources of aid to aviation education programs. Such publications may also offer clues as to aviation interests in a particular community. Sometimes a local aviation activity employs an educational consultant, or at least someone charged with public relations responsibilities who can be of assistance to local school people.

COOPERATIVE COMMUNITY SERVICES

The classroom use of the services discussed in the following paragraphs imposes a definite responsibility upon educators. The teacher, the teaching staff, and the school system must retain the right to evaluate materials and services offered in terms of their educational appropriateness. Such a program of evaluation must be continuous. Should materials or services not meet approved standards, they should not be recommended for student use.

Not all of the cooperative community services discussed in the succeeding paragraphs will be available in every locality. For this very reason, the scope of the services suggested has been kept in broad groupings. In chapter v there will be found a more specific listing of many resources.

The materials and services available from cooperating community agencies for use in the instructional program fall generally into four categories: (1) resource people; (2) field trips or school excursions; (3) other audio-visual aids; (4) printed materials. These four groupings will be discussed briefly in turn.

Resource people constitute an infinitely rich and varied source of information, assistance, and stimulation wherever aviation touches the school curriculum. Teachers and school administrators in their search for resource people will naturally turn primarily to the aviation industry itself—its factories, scheduled and nonscheduled airlines, airports, fixed-base operators, training schools, and the like. Within these groupings the number of people who can contribute effectively to classroom work in aviation education is indeed large.

A second group of people who are in position to contribute to the instructional program, are those government officials attached to aviation agencies. On the federal level there are the Civil Aeronautics Board and the Civil Aeronautics Administration. These agencies have regional offices throughout the United States. At the state level, there are the officials of the state aeronautical agency. Such agencies are variously named in different parts of the country. At the metropolitan, municipal, and town level, there are frequently officials concerned with airport management, and with government control of aviation in and near the metropolitan area.

Excursions, field trips, and school journeys are available to the resourceful teacher in a wide range of possibilities. A trip to the airport is the activity most frequently used. Trips through factories, through service hangars, armed forces installations, are also frequently utilized. Visits to public hearings on aviation matters, conducted by federal, state, and local governing bodies, can provide the class with insights into the complex problems of aviation development.

The techniques useful in conducting field trips have been dealt with in such books as Edgar Dale, *Audio-Visual Methods in Teaching*.[2] The reader is referred to these books for guidance. With respect to airport and factory field trips, however, the experience of many teachers suggests that par-

[2] Dale, *Audio-Visual Methods in Teaching* (New York: Dryden Press, 1946.)

ticular attention should be given to two matters: (1) The complexity of the modern airport and factory suggests that several visits for limited and intensive study may be more fruitful than a "bird's eye view" of the entire operation. (2) The great variety of experiences available suggests that the resourceful teacher accommodate the individual differences in his class by sending small groups of pupils on different trips to different installations.

The entire range of audio-visual materials is available from one or another of the community aviation resources. In another chapter, this will be dealt with in greater detail. It will be sufficient here to indicate the variety of materials known to be available; (1) models and mock-ups of airplanes, airports, engines, instruments, etc.; (2) motion picture films on all aspects of the aviation industry, slides, pictures, and filmstrips; (3) maps, globes, graphs, and charts; (4) records and recordings.

Printed materials of many kinds and on a wide range of subjects are available. In addition to brochures and booklets, teachers will find much of value for particular purposes in airline timetables and tables of fares between airports. Careful evaluation of this material is, of course, necessary to select that which is appropriate to the reading ability and the interest of the group with which it is to be used.

The Problem of Establishing Liaison with Cooperative Groups

Many community aviation interests, as indicated elsewhere, are available as cooperating interests. These can be approached in accordance with established school policy. Schools and aviation agencies should find a common area of purpose which makes cooperation mutually desirable, reasonable, and beneficial. The establishing of school-community liaison is the responsibility of the schools.

Before attempting to enlist the educational service of a cooperating agency, steps should be taken to learn what services are available and whether or not they are educationally justifiable. Next, it is important to define the purposes of such service. The third step includes explaining the program of cooperation to those concerned, and presenting this in terms of common purposes to be achieved.

The following paragraph offers for consideration an outline of proven liaison procedure:

Appointment of a special educational representative by a school administrator. This representative, either a member of the staff or an able faculty member, be he teacher or supervisor, is the leader in aviation education. He should be delegated responsibility for the proper coordination of the cooperative program. The representative should compile and classify a reliable list of community resources, and make this list available for use by all school personnel. He should establish contact with appropriate agency representatives so that he may determine the types of services available and plan how they may be used. He should guide the many and varied education opportunities offered by community interests into educational channels. He should encourage, at frequent intervals, evaluation of the cooperative services provided. Such evaluation is a function of teacher and pupil under the guidance of the supervisor. He should report to cooperating agencies evaluation results and suggestions made for improvement of the program based upon such appraisals. He should nurture and cultivate contacts with community agencies once they are established.

An advisory committee composed of community representatives, school personnel, and representatives from each cooperating group should prove helpful to school representatives whose task is to maintain liaison between school and cooperating agencies.

Summary

It is important that educational leadership make the best possible use of national, state, and local cooperating agencies. Before this can be done, the person in a school system charged with assisting teacher or instructor in a supervisory or guidance capacity must take preliminary steps to assure smooth functioning of the cooperative program. He must ascertain the nature and location of extraschool educational services. He should direct the development and application of criteria for use in determining the appropriateness of such services, particularly as they relate to instructional materials. He should undertake to establish harmonious relationships with cooperative groups. He should guide his teachers and instructors as they use the educational services of industry, government, or other agency so that effective and cooperative working relationships are maintained.

4. Community Aviation Education

THE FUTURE OF AMERICA is in the making *now*, in the minds of its citizens—people on the streets, in homes, factories, offices, and schools. The impact of aviation upon the lives of people is a factor in shaping their thinking. Aviation education must consequently take steps to assure that this impact is exactly understood.

One way to bring about adult understanding of aviation— its benefits and its hazards—is to involve as many segments of the community as possible (1) in recognizing problems of the air age, (2) in studying and working out solutions to these and (3) in planning the future in terms of these solutions.

Aviation has revolutionized communications and transportation. It has opened new avenues to scientific pursuit, industrial enterprise, and vocational opportunity.

A world confronted by changing concepts of time and space faces economic and social problems which break with tradition. The impact of these forces on the way of life in a community is tremendous and makes imperative action and leadership for aviation education in each community.

Opportunities for community activities which produce an enlightened public must be recognized; leadership must be employed which will capitalize on such opportunities. These leaders must learn how to involve the layman in community programs of adult aviation education; they must use these programs to bring to the post-school citizen a full comprehension of the circumstances of the aviation age. Such adult education services can be best planned and administered through the extension services of organized education.

Opportunity for Community-wide
Aviation Education

Adult participation in aviation education has two major purposes. One of these is to acquaint the public with the more important everyday problems of aviation. The other is to enlist the aid of the well-informed layman and the organization he represents in the interest of organized education as it guides the community youth in understanding consequent problems.

Aviation demands new social understandings. The advent of the high speed large cargo transport has produced an exchange of people and ideas unparalleled by any single event in all history. Along with the rapid "shrinking" of world trade routes comes an almost equally rapid rise in international trade and commerce. Today the names of such cities as Teheran, Tunis, and Karachi are as familiar to us as those of Topeka and Peoria. People are beginning to understand that the trip from Chicago to Moscow is not made by going east through New York, but rather by taking the short route over Hudson Bay and the tip of Greenland. Thinking of global navigation in another way, our citizens are beginning to understand that our industrial centers of Chicago-Detroit-Cleveland are as vulnerable to air attack as New York-Philadelphia-Baltimore. In short, we are living in and experiencing an era of unprecedented change brought about by one of man's most important inventions. Unfortunately, our social understanding has not kept pace with our technological advances, and this invention, to some extent, already has created problems for which we must find solutions.

Community organizations offer opportunity for aviation-age orientation. In order to help with the solutions to the problems created by aviation, the aviation education leader will have at his command several organizations, ideally suited for the task. Among these are Rotary, Kiwanis, and other service clubs, civic organizations, professional clubs, the public schools, the local aviation industries, and airport officials. These civic or professional groups, through available public relations media, can answer many of the questions raised by both civil and military aviation.

Outlined below is a list of aviation topics requiring a better public understanding; other topics of interest will occur to the reader.

1. Cost, need, and benefits of airport expansion programs
2. Global geography and other new aviation concepts
3. Regulation and controls—CAA, CAB, state, and the like
4. Need for aviation research and development
5. Hazards in aviation and safety measures
6. Private flying
7. Increased landing speed: runways and traffic patterns
8. The taxpayer and the cost of an aviation program
9. Aviation and the national defense

Public understanding of the areas listed above is essential to the future of aviation. It is important that they be given public consideration.

The air-youth movement offers an excellent means of stimulating adult interest in a youth-service program. Through supporting the air-youth movement, the uninitiated among the grown-ups are motivated to learn something of the nature of the movement they support. Those adults already informed concerning aviation can provide guidance, supervision, and technical assistance. They should be urged to contribute time to such programs as the Air Scouts, Wing Scouts, model clubs, flying and soaring clubs, and the Cadet Program of the Civil Air Patrol. Youth movements need the assistance and guidance of technically and scientifically trained people. Young people have great respect for the opinions of experts; consequently, when a youth group discusses flying, a pilot should act as the group leader. When discussing the problem of communications, an electronics expert should be assigned the task.

To accomplish the objectives of the air-youth program the combined resources of the community should be used. Such resources may include its public schools, nearby military establishments, and local industry. Each of these groups has a particular service to offer.

How the Aviation Education Leader Serves Community Groups

The aviation education leader can effectively serve community aviation activities in three major ways: (*a*) by active participation as an authority, (*b*) by providing liaison service, and (*c*) by promotional activities.

He must be an active participant in the aviation activities of the community. As a leader he can foster aviation education in the organizations—civic, service, and professional— of the community by serving on aviation and education committees of the various groups. He should belong to clubs concerned directly with aviation—aero clubs, model clubs, and the like. He should participate, as a representative of aviation, in hearings or discussions concerning or affecting aviation or aviation interests before governmental agencies. The ability of the leader to show interest, enthusiasm, and the willingness to work will encourage interest and participation by others.

The aviation education leader should be able to supply information when needed. As a consultant he should maintain a bibliography of material and a library of visual materials. He should be currently informed in both aviation and community activities. He should offer his services as adviser, speaker, and teacher, and provide the names of others who can render like service.

Because of the leader's educational background and abilities he is ideally fitted to establish liaison between groups within the community; to coordinate the efforts of educational, governmental, commercial, and service club organizations; and to contact state, national, and international groups. The organization of an advisory group in community-wide aviation education with a representative membership can become an initial step toward coordination of the aviation education activities within the community. Liaison between local, state, national, and international groups and agencies can be established either through correspondence or by direct contact, and developed through subsequent meetings, institutes, and workshops.

The initiation of community aviation education activities is a leadership function. An aviation education leader should be a promoter. He should, by initiative and imagination, originate programs of aviation education activities. He can publicize these activities by preparing and distributing material to newspapers, periodicals, and radio and television stations, preparing and producing radio and television plays, demonstrations, and panel discussions.

An important phase of promotion is the enlisting of sponsors and obtaining financial backing for community projects. By maintaining close contact with commercial and industrial interests, the leader can ensure that many of these efforts receive material support. The aviation education leader should inaugurate programs of aviation education in his community; assist in the conduct of programs initiated; promote and publicize these programs; coordinate the community's efforts; and establish working relationships among cooperating interests and agencies.

How to Enlist Appropriate Community Groups

Community aviation interests can be classified as: commercial, educational, recreational, and civic. The commercial aviation interests are aware of the value of good public relations. Education is directly involved in community service. Groups organized for recreational purposes should be eager to include aviation among their activities. Civic organizations, by their very nature, are vitally interested in all community activities. In order to encourage the active participation of such groups, aviation education leadership will employ a logical approach.

In the light of international developments and the part played by aviation in these, enlightenment on aviation matters should be speedily brought to our adult population. These questions arise: How can this tremendous task be accomplished within the limitations of our democratic structure in the shortest possible time and to the greatest possible extent? What should be taught to increase general aviation enlightenment? Through what mediums may such enlightenments and subsequent understanding be gained and employed? What methods of instruction will be apropos? What will such a program cost, and how can it be financed?

Interest is directly proportionate to a realization of need; consequently, realization of a need for aviation education must be established on the basis that such programs are timely and pertinent. To so establish these realizations and promote interest in satisfying such needs, a survey committee composed of representatives of aviation interests should be formed. Active participation in the founding of an organized effort develops the proprietary interest of the participant. After the survey is completed, groups represented on the committee can be guided by the leader to assume additional aviation education responsibilities.

Interest can be further increased by establishing a program for the interchange of information. The opportunity to publicize an activity program is generally welcomed enthusiastically. Exchange of speakers for meetings, school-industry visitations, cooperative projects between industry and education, the development of work-experience programs, the preparation of teaching aids and devices for instructional use, and encouragement of participation by agencies outside the school, all these are methods the aviation education leader will employ.

A most effective means that has proven its merit is the luncheon meeting. Leaders of all community agencies interested in aviation should be invited. The invitation should clearly state the objectives of the meeting, and state the topic under consideration. This should be of community-wide interest. It might be chosen from among the following: airport planning and zoning; airplane noise; aviation education; aviation's implication for property values; aviation hazards; transportation problems to and from airports; airport facilities and aviation appropriations (local, state, national). The agenda to be followed during the meeting period should be outlined. At the meeting a key aviation education leader might well be invited to speak on the social, economic, political, and technological implications of aviation and of its impact on the community.

The following are suggested as local industries and agencies that should be invited to send a key official to such a meeting with local educators: *airlines*, both scheduled and nonscheduled; *military establishments*, Air Force, Navy, and Civil Air Patrol; *federal agencies:* Civil Aeronautics Administration, Weather Bureau, and Communications; the *state department of aeronautics; professional aviation organizations* such as the Aviation Transport Association, National Aviation Trades Association, Association of Airport Operators, Association of Airport Executives, and the National Aeronautic Association; and *local groups* including airport commissions, aviation commissions, the chamber of commerce, state and local school administrators, airport operators, flight operators, manufacturers and suppliers of aircraft and equipment, fixed-base operators, aviation clubs, newspapers, radio and television stations and churches.

A survey of the community's aviation problems might be

planned, and at the initial luncheon meeting a committee could be set up to undertake the survey, study the problems it reveals, and suggest solutions to these problems. Another committee would determine the economic contribution being made to the community by aviation. It is suggested that this latter committee explore and report upon the following:

1. Number and types of the community's airports
2. Value of airport facilities
3. Number of aircraft being operated and their total value
    a) Airline
    b) Executive
    c) Fixed-Base
    d) Private
4. Number of manufacturers and suppliers of aircraft, material and supplies
5. Number of persons employed locally in aviation and their average earnings[1]

Public aviation education forums should follow initial meetings. Those attending the first meeting should be urged by the leader to participate in follow-up programs, making available their resources in material and personnel in helping to develop general public understandings of aviation's role in community progress. Such follow-up programs may be planned as a forum, with a moderator and at least a four-member panel. Each member of the panel should be assigned one of the topics investigated by the committees selected at the organization meeting.

It is hardly necessary to point out the need for communicating with community, church, and political leaders and encouraging their participation in the community aviation education program. In all instances, the initiative for the organization of these meetings should be taken by a representative of the local school administration.

[1] See p. 51 for other suggested topics.

APPROACHES TO ADULT EDUCATION PROGRAMS IN AVIATION

Adults, unlike children, are not required by law to attend school; consequently, adult aviation education enjoys no captive audiences. However, there are several media through which pertinent aviation information may be disseminated and aviation understandings reached. Among these are the following: (1) public and private school adult education courses in Aviation and the Modern World; [2] (2) programs by citizen groups for the promotion of aviation; such groups include service clubs, civic clubs, chambers of commerce, labor groups, and local aviation industry groups; (3) newspaper and magazine stories, and radio and television programs.

Perhaps the most effective approach could be made through the program committee of a community's service club. The board of education could make available to such committees the services of the aviation education supervisor who as a lecturer would schedule a series of addresses covering the major aspects of aviation.

Someone has to initiate a program of this kind, and someone has to do the work and assume the initiative; otherwise little will be done. The community's school system through its aviation education supervisor will need to assume this responsibility.

The aviation industry and other interests should join organized education in sponsoring the adult education program. An industry-education advisory committee should be formed to help plan courses to be offered or activity to be undertaken. A subdivision of such a committee can help with the problem of finance.

Millions of dollars are appropriated each year for adult education by states and local boards of education. This money goes for salaries of administrators, supervisors, teach-

[2] Offered by University of Illinois and other leading colleges and universities.

ers of adult educational courses, institutes, instructional supplies, and special teaching aids. Adult education is interested in rendering the maximum public service and in cooperating with representative groups of citizens and industry in providing for adult educational needs in the communities and states in which they are employed. However, prior to setting up adult education programs, the need for a given program must be demonstrated. This means that a harmony of understanding must be developed among those engaged in the aviation business, including local leaders of the aviation industry and CAA representatives, and the appropriate adult education authorities. Since it is unlikely that any of these groups will take the first steps toward reaching such understanding without outside encouragement, the aviation education supervisor again comes into the picture. He and his committee should bring these interests together and help plan the courses in aviation and aviation understanding subsequently offered.

IMPLEMENTATION AND ORIENTATION DEVICES

Aviation education leaders who are in charge of planning community activities with adults will find it desirable and worth while to acquaint themselves with various implementation and orientation services which will assist them in successfully launching their programs.

Flying clubs

In a number of communities flying clubs are in successful operation. Enthusiastic groups of progressive air-minded people are learning to fly at airports throughout the country, in club-owned ships, at moderate cost. This is an approach to adult aviation education which must not be neglected. Aviation education leaders may obtain, upon request to the Aviation Information Office, Civil Aeronautics Administration, a booklet entitled *The Flying Club* which tells about the organization and operation of such clubs.

The air marking program

Air marking is an undertaking which can be employed to stimulate community-wide interest in aviation. Community leaders will be eager to seize upon the opportunity that air marking offers to get the community's name upon the map. Information concerning the air marking program and aid in putting such a program into effect can be obtained from the Office of Federal Airways of the Civil Aeronautics Administration.

Other implementing devices

Following is a suggestive list of other implementing devices for an aviation education program, and how to use them:

1. *Newspapers.*—Send a continuous flow of news items to the local dailies as well as the community papers.

2. *Movie film trailers.*—Develop movie film trailers to advertise air-age activities and get local theaters to screen these at the breaks in their regular programs.

3. *Posters.*—Have school art departments make posters on aviation education activities. Induce prominent stores to give free window space for their display.

4. *Radio.*—Arrange with local radio stations to make spot announcements.

5. *Television.*—Work with television station script writers to produce an aviation education TV presentation.

6. *Airport tours.*—Arrange for guided tours for adult groups through the local airport facilities, weather bureau, control tower, and maintenance hangars. Schedule short special air trips for those who have never flown.

7. *Aircraft manufacturing plant visits.*—Take adult groups

on inspection visits to aircraft plants in the area to see airplanes being built.

8. *Open house nights at schools.*—Arrange for periodic open house and exhibit nights at vocational and technical schools that teach aviation courses to give the general public an opportunity to see school shops and laboratories in operation.

9. *School auditorium meetings.*—Invite aviation leaders from local plants, airports, and airlines to address groups of young adults. Have a forum discussion following the lectures.

10. *Service clubs.*—Arrange to speak on "Aviation Education" before Rotary, Kiwanis, Lions, Gyro, Optimist, Exchange, and other service clubs. Also—PTA's, church brotherhoods, fraternal lodges, etc. Get local aero club to assist in planning these meetings.

11. *Aircraft exhibits.*—Set up aircraft exhibits in lobbies of public buildings, where many people pass by, such as the city hall, county building, chamber of commerce, public library, and prominent clubs.

12. *County fairs, automobile shows, and Better Home and Garden expositions.*—Have display booths assigned for purpose of aviation education exhibits.

13. *Automatic stereopticon slide projectors.*—Where they are available, use automatic stereopticon slide projectors with sets of aviation slides and have continuous automatic projection on daylight screens at fairs, shows, and expositions.

14. *Printed bulletins, brochures, and pamphlets.*—Prepare material for printing and where possible have this printed in vocational school printing and lithographic shops. Arrange for general distribution at public meetings, on office "counter literature racks," near time clocks in plants and places of employment, on airport bulletin boards, in clubs, Boy Scout headquarters, church, YMCA, and on announcement boards

of Legion and veteran posts, labor union meeting halls, lodge halls, and many other places where people congregate.

SUMMARY

In view of the changing conditions of the times, which in great part have come about because of aviation's social and military effects and which certainly can be symbolized by aviation, it becomes important that the services of the nation's schools extend aviation education to the adult citizens of its communities. The security of the nation may well depend upon the speed with which its citizenry, in school or out, actually comprehends aviation's potential and then does something about it.

This means that the supervisor or leader in aviation education must seize every opportunity for working with adult groups in his community. He must encourage and perhaps direct formalized offerings in adult education by his municipal school system, and yet he must do much more than this. He must initiate and conduct programs of aviation education for community organizations in which interest can be stimulated. He must employ every communication device to get his message across. In these efforts he will have the cooperation of many interests. It is worthy of note that a by-product of the community aviation education program may well be greater harmony of understanding between school and community, with both school and community fully realizing the necessity of the recriprocal service necessary if the community's educational program is to reach its peak of highest efficiency.

5. Agencies and Interests Providing Aviation Education Services

THERE ARE MANY organizations throughout the nation which provide instructional materials which include information about a given field of human activity, and teachers have used many materials provided by these services. Airlines, aircraft manufacturers, aviation organizations, and governmental bureaus are sources from which free and low-cost materials can be obtained. These materials can fill the gaps between the actual developments and subsequently published textual material—a gap which often amounts to as much as five years. During the past two or three years the aforementioned groups have supplied the schools of the country with copious supplies of materials. However, budgetary problems have recently made it necessary for these organizations to reduce both their production and distribution.

The following national organizations employ aviation education advisers and furnish information and printed materials:

Academy of Model Aeronautics, 1025 Connecticut Avenue, N.W., Washington 6, D.C.; Russell Nichols, Executive Director

Air Transport Association of America, 1107 Sixteenth Street, N.W., Washington 6, D.C.; Elmer Thompson, Vice-President–Director of Information

American Airlines, Kenneth E. Newland, Educational Director, c/o Stephens College, Columbia, Mo.

Civil Aeronautics Administration, Washington 25, D.C.; Harold E. Mehrens, Deputy Director, Aviation Education Staff

Civil Air Patrol, Bolling Air Force Base, Washington 25, D.C.; Mervin K. Strickler, Aviation Educationist

Pan-American World Airways, 28-19 Bridge Plaza North, Long
Island City, N.Y.; George Gardner, Educational Director

Trans World Airlines, 80 East 42nd Street, New York, N.Y.; John
H. Furbay, Director, Air World Education

United Air Lines, 5959 South Cicero Avenue, Chicago 38, Ill.;
Ray O. Mertes, Director, School and College Service

University Aviation Association, Parks College of St. Louis University, East St. Louis, Ill.; Gene Kropf, President

U.S. Air Force, Office of Public Information, Room 4-C-962,
Pentagon, Washington, D.C.; Major K. D. McFarland, Chief,
Special Events Branch, Liaison Division

U.S. Department of the Navy, Office of Information, Room 4-D-
718, Pentagon, Washington, D.C.; Lt. Comdr. Howard B. Eddy,
Assistant Head, Civilian Organizations and Ceremonies Branch

U.S. Office of Education, Department of Health, Education and
Welfare, Washington 25, D.C.; Willis C. Brown, Specialist for
Aviation Education.

Materials

Among items such agencies prepare for school use, those
most common are printed materials and audio-visual aids.
If these are properly used, they bring the child closer to
everyday living, create interest in the modern commercial
world, provide up-to-date information not now available in
textbooks, enrich class discussions, and help students learn to
locate a wide variety of source materials.

One of the sources of information used by many teachers
is the teacher's manual. The purpose of this aid is not primarily to give factual data on a particular subject, but to
suggest classroom activities which will uncover the information desired. Although many facts are given, both verbally
and pictorially, in the materials, it is recognized that teachers
will have to employ other aids and devices.

Teacher kits, put out by several airline companies, in some
instances contain a variety of visual aids of value to the
teacher who is concerned with developing a better under-

standing of our world neighbors. They may also provide unifying and supplementary textual materials to facilitate maximum utilization of these aids. They always indicate the important contributions made by air transportation in bringing about closer social and economic relationships between the United States and other countries.

Available sound films prove to be instructional aids of primary importance. In this area, films are still needed which will help children on the several maturity levels to understand important air-age concepts. Firsthand experiences such as observing an airport in operation may have educational value beyond the indirect experience of reading about the activities carried on there. When direct experiences are not possible, models and mock-ups found in the aviation education center or fabricated during a "free-activity" period may be employed. Opportunities are sometimes available for industrial experiences through "earn-learn" programs. These, of course, are limited to older students who are permitted by law to participate.

It should be understood that much of the material provided by industry, agencies, services, and government bureaus has been developed for public relations or for technical purposes. Regardless of the purposes for which these materials are prepared, they will, if carefully selected and wisely used, provide understanding of current scientific and sociological developments that is not at present found in the pages of many textbooks.

Materials of instruction should be examined, modified, and supplemented in order to bring them up-to-date from a factual and scientific standpoint. All materials must be previewed and given an appropriate grade index. There is no justification for using any materials or firsthand experiences so advanced as to contribute nothing to a given learning situation. This applies to such materials as globes, air-age maps, charts, graphs, pictures, slides, models, instruments and diagrams, and textual materials.

Much of the material received by teachers from industry is of the general information type. In some cases this is immediately usable. In other cases, teachers must exert considerable effort in order to adapt it to classroom use.

ENCOURAGING THE PREPARATION OF INSTRUCTIONAL MATERIALS

Once a program of aviation education is decided upon, the teacher's most immediate need is for materials of instruction: printed material, films, and instructional devices. The basic sources of these materials are from (a) educational publishers, (b) government agencies: federal, state, and local, (c) the armed services, (d) commercial concerns, (e) aviation industry, (f) civic or service groups, (g) qualified individuals, and (h) a combination of any or all of the above. There are several classifications into which aviation education materials may fall. There are those materials to be prepared specifically for aviation education use. Other items prepared for education generally can be employed in aviation education. Some technical training material developed for use in aviation trade schools can also be used, in part, at least, in the general aviation education program. The aviation industry's public relations and advertising materials are often quite usable. The technical aviation materials such as reports, papers, and engineering studies can be used at certain levels. The miscellaneous materials will range from commercial aviation publications to fiction and comic books.

The schools themselves must take the lead in producing aviation education materials. Educators and leaders may encourage the preparation of needed materials by several methods. Perhaps the most logical approach is simply to publicize the needs that exist. If material is not available or suitable, such condition should be brought to the attention of publishers or other producers. Publishers of texts and materials, as well as the audio-visual aids producers, are sensitive to teacher demand. It is evident that these people will eventually produce the needed materials, although there will necessarily be a considerable time lag between the apparent need and the filling of that need.

School administrators have found that some of their teachers are already preparing aviation education aids. It is suggested that an effort be made to discover such undertakings, and that teachers be encouraged to submit their contributions to a publisher. If the nature of the material produced by such teacher does not warrant its publication by a commercial concern, it should be brought to the attention of such agencies as the city, county, or state education department, the state aviation commission, the Civil Aeronautics Administration, or a representative aviation industry.

Schools will discover a good public relations device to be the producing of limited quantities of their own aviation education programs, units, and activities and making selected distribution to other schools, interested agencies, and to the press. Every effort should be made to include stimulating information in state department of education courses of study. Individual schools and colleges should employ workshop activities in the production of such materials of instruction. The help of both state aviation commissions and the Civil Aeronautics Administration should be enlisted in such workshop situations. Many schools have their own audio-visual departments. With a minimum of encouragement these will prepare motion pictures, filmstrips, slides, and photographs appropriate for use in programs of aviation education.

Perhaps the greatest potential for the preparation of instructional materials is the aviation industry itself. Both the air transport and the aircraft manufacturing segments of the industry are aware of not only the schools' needs in this respect, but also the tremendous stake the industry has in the nation's schools. Industry, like other cooperating groups, is seeking help with this materials of instruction problem. Perhaps the best stimulation that aviation education leadership can give to the task of preparing materials of instruction is to lend a helping hand in planning and preparing them, and thus assure both producer and user that materials when prepared will be appropriate and, consequently, can be employed advantageously. The importance of continually producing good materials cannot be overemphasized. It is through them that the busy teacher is able to supply his students with all the answers to their questions.

Some larger cities maintain an aviation center for the city school system at large. For others, however, it is more practical to think in terms of individual school aviation-library centers. A given senior high school, for instance, may well develop an individual center which could serve its own area as a nucleus for a group of junior high and elementary grade schools. The services of the aviation teacher-librarian and the facilities of the aviation center should be available to all teachers and pupils of such an area, regardless of subject departments or grade levels. As the center grows, it may come to have an aviation instructor in charge who may use it daily for one or more high school aviation classes.

In some states (California, Indiana, Kansas, Oklahoma, and Texas) a mobile air center program has been tried out on an experimental basis. An itinerary is carefully planned, generally on a city-wide or county-wide basis. The mobile unit usually includes expert consultant service and may include some of the following items of equipment:

Mock-ups
Charts
Aircraft instruments
Models

Maps
Globes
Navigation computers
Meteorological equipment
Engine and/or engine parts
Aircraft parts
A Link demonstrator or other device for demonstrating aircraft
  controls
A Link Trainer
Pictures of airplanes
Books, pamphlets, and other printed materials on all aspects
  of aviation: (a) the nature of aviation; (b) the social,
  political, and economic impact of aviation on society; (c)
  interest groups, official and nonofficial; (d) technical aviation;
  (e) aviation as a vocation

Demonstrations are given to groups of teachers and pupils.
In this manner aviation help can be offered in all fields and
on all levels. The mobile unit serves as an air center for one,
two, or three days in a given school.

INTERPRETATION OF MATERIALS PREPARED
BY INDUSTRY

The aviation industry publishes a great variety of materials
for distribution among the adult population with a view
toward "sales" promotion. With some imagination and
planning, a clever teacher can use these aids to good advantage. In cases where textbooks are fairly adequate, these
materials are helpful in enriching and bringing content up
to date. Included in such resources are house organs, trade
journals, newsletters, magazines, handbooks, time schedules,
films, filmstrips, pamphlets, and many other types of material.
Since most of these materials are of an advertising nature,
the teacher must be able to select those which will make a
significant contribution to educational objectives, and to
eliminate those which are largely promotional. Much can
be said for the teacher orienting himself in the limitations

and possibilities of these resources; however, a very effective device would be to have pupils assemble, organize, and evaluate the aids in terms of their appropriateness for the on-going project.

Most of the materials produced by industry are too difficult for the lower elementary grades. Nevertheless, there are numerous ways in which these aids can be used. An effective method would be for the teacher to rewrite certain materials. In a school system which houses both the elementary and secondary schools, a good project for a secondary group is to have them put into understandable language some of these aids for use by elementary pupils. Some companies prepare teacher guides that will give help in adapting materials for use in the classroom.

Many of the materials developed for the general public are not too difficult in readability for upper elementary and secondary pupils. Discrimination in selecting materials can be a stimulating activity for pupils. In guiding the pupils in intelligent use of these aids, the following questions might prove valuable:

1. Is the writer an authority in his field?
2. Will the material achieve the purposes for which the teacher intends it?
3. Is it fair in the presentation of controversial matters?
4. Is it well illustrated?
5. Is it attractive?
6. Is it written in a straightforward manner?
7. Is it timely?
8. Does it conceal or exaggerate?
9. Does it live up to the standards of decency and fair play?

There are also highly technical materials available which can be used to good advantage in the more specialized phases of instruction. At times, whether on the technical or nontechnical level, company representatives will agree to come in as resource persons to interpret their materials. Through public relations offices, teachers may suggest to industrial concerns ways in which they could improve their materials, thereby making them more effective for the general public, especially for school use.

BIBLIOGRAPHIES OF AVIATION MATERIALS

The following list should be found of value to the aviation education supervisor. The items listed should be made readily available to him and his teachers. The supervisor will find that each bibliography described below contains the names of books, pamphlets, films, and other instructional aids which should be at his and his teachers' disposal.

PARKS COLLEGE OF AERONAUTICAL TECHNOLOGY, ST. LOUIS UNIVERSITY. *100 Air-Age Films Available to Schools and Colleges from Industry.* East St. Louis, Ill.: Parks College of Aeronautical Technology. 16 pp. Gratis.

A partial listing of 16mm, sound films available from industry and other sources that may be used in furthering air-age and aviation education. Only a few of the films available from the CAA, the U.S. Air Force, and the U.S. Navy are included. The film list is organized into three sections; namely, aircraft and equipment, general aviation, and travel.

UNITED AIR LINES, SCHOOL AND COLLEGE SERVICE. *Free Aviation Education Materials and Services.* Chicago: United Air Lines, School and College Service, 35 East Monroe St., 1952. Folder. Gratis.

A listing of the various aviation education teaching aids available through United Air Lines. Besides publications designed specifically for school use, slidefilms, motion picture films, and bulletin board pictures are listed. An order form is attached to the folder by means of which the items listed may be ordered merely by checking appropriate blanks.

U.S. DEPARTMENT OF HEALTH, EDUCATION AND WELFARE, OFFICE OF EDUCATION, DIVISION OF SECONDARY EDUCATION. *Government Aeronautical Services, Publications, and Visual Aids Available to Teachers.* (Circular No. 331). Washington:

Department of Health, Education and Welfare, Office of Education, January 1952. 10 pp. Gratis.

A complete listing of the aeronautical resources available from government agencies for the use of teachers of elementary and secondary schools. This information is arranged in three sections: services, publications, and visual aids. Under each section is given a brief description of the offerings of these agencies, whether there is a charge for the service or publication, and how and where it is available.

U.S. GOVERNMENT PRINTING OFFICE. *Aviation, PL 79.* Washington: Superintendent of Documents, U.S. Government Printing Office, February 1950. 24 pp. Gratis.

A complete listing revised periodically, of all government publications relating to aviation. Included are publications of the Air Force, the Navy, the CAA, the CAB, and the many technical reports of the National Advisory Committee for Aeronautics. Also included are reports of various congressional committees dealing with aviation. Several order blanks for use in ordering publications listed are attached to the bulletin.

OKLAHOMA AVIATION COMMISSION. *Air-Age Teaching Materials.* Oklahoma City: Oklahoma Aviation Commission, Route 6, Box 249. Folder. Gratis.

A miscellaneous listing of sources of materials, and also listings available from the Oklahoma Aviation Commission and other sources, of bulletins, texts, pictures, magazines, and miscellaneous items useful to teachers.

OKLAHOMA AVIATION COMMISSION. *Sources of Aviation Materials You Need.* Oklahoma City: Oklahoma Aviation Commission, Route 6, Box 249. Folder. Gratis.

A listing of the major sources of aviation teaching materials, including airlines, governmental agencies, and commercial aviation concerns. Also listed are most of the aviation periodicals and magazines, as well as a list of publications and films available from the Oklahoma Aviation Commission.

U.S. OFFICE OF EDUCATION. *Aviation Periodicals for Teachers and Pupils.* Washington: Department of Health, Education, and Welfare. Circular #381, January 1954. 6 pp. Gratis.

A list of periodicals recommended by a group of teachers for school use.

U.S. CIVIL AERONAUTICS ADMINISTRATION. *Aviation Education Sources—Free and Low-Cost Materials.* Washington: Civil Aeronautics Administration, Aviation Education Division, April 1952. 10 pp. Gratis.

A listing of sources of aviation materials for general classroom use, broken down by subject and by alphabetical list of sources. Also included are appendices listing materials currently available upon request from the CAA Aviation Education Division, a general list of CAA publications, and a listing of the Civil Air Regulations published by the CAB.

U.S. CIVIL AERONAUTICS ADMINISTRATION. *Film Bibliography of Aviation and Related Fields.* Washington: Superintendent of Documents, U.S. Government Printing Office, 1949. 91 pp. $0.40.

A bibliography, with annotations, of films and filmstrips useful in aviation education available from all sources, commercial as well as governmental. The bulletin is broken down into an annotated listing of films, index of films by subject and title, and an alphabetical index of film sources.

U.S. CIVIL AERONAUTICS ADMINISTRATION. *List of Publications.* Washington: Civil Aeronautics Administration, Office of Aviation Information, 1952. (Also available from the Aviation Education Division, CAA). 10 pp. Gratis.

An annotated listing, revised semi-annually, of all publications of the CAA. These publications deal with the subjects of airports, aviation education, aeronautical training, and miscellaneous aeronautical subjects. Also included is a listing of currently available A.N.C. Bulletins (Air Force, Navy, and Civil Aeronautics Administration).

SUMMARY

The one assigned supervisory responsibility over the community-wide aviation education program must find assistance of many types if he is to approach success in his task. He will need to make use of local, state, and national organizations and agencies. He must discover the resources of his community and arrange for the best possible use of these resources. In some instances it will be necessary for him to encourage and to participate in interpreting "adult level" material for the immature student. He will enlist help in the preparation of instructional materials in aviation from those teachers who work with him. Above all he will be informed concerning sources from which teachers and students can obtain those materials relevant to their aviation education purposes. Many instructional materials, aids, and devices will have been assembled by him and made available to students and teachers through the aviation education center.

6. Seven Significant Trends
in Curriculum Improvement

IN JUNE OF 1950 a study was inaugurated to determine the degree of interest in aviation education manifested by school systems throughout the United States. The study was conducted by a committee of the American Association of School Administrators with funds made available by the Civil Aeronautics Administration.

The first phase of the study was undertaken by Herbert B. Bruner, chairman of the Committee on Aviation Education of the American Association of School Administrators. An analysis of information which he gathered regarding the place of aviation education in thirty-two school systems in cities of over 100,000 population revealed that aviation education centers around six trends in curriculum improvement:

1. Toward a better understanding of child growth and development, and the recognition of interest, purpose, and experience as important factors in learning.

2. Toward the recognition of the school's responsibility to help students understand the complex age in which they live, and through guided experience to help them to assume responsibility for the improvement of life.

3. Toward a growing realization of the school's responsibility to education for vocational competence and to help youth choose a career.

4. Toward a more integrated organization of the curriculum and the use of the large center of interest as a frame of reference.

Toward recognition of the school's responsibility to help students understand the complex age in which they live (Trend 2). A fifth grade in Colorado sees lobster just flown in from Alaska.

Above: Toward a growing realization of the school's responsibility to educate for vocational competence (Trend 3).

Below: Toward a more integrated organization of the curriculum, and the use of the large center of interest as a frame of reference (Trend 4).

Toward a wider use of community and school resources as aids to learning
(Trend 5). A fifth grade visits the communications room at the airport.

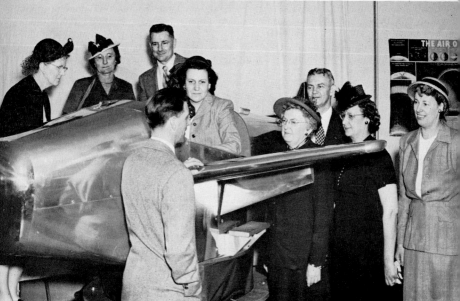

Above: Toward the acceptance of in-service education as an integral aspect of curriculum improvement (Trend 6).

Below: Toward extending the service of organized education to the adults of the community (Trend 7). A state department of education aviation consultant talks to teachers who have just returned from a flight.

5. Toward a wider use of community resources as aids to learning: for example, the field trip and participation in neighborhood projects.

6. Toward the acceptance of in-service education of teachers as a permanent need of the schools and as an integral aspect of curriculum improvement.

The second phase of the study involved 300 school systems representing all geographical areas in the United States, and all types of American communities. A questionnaire was prepared by the AASA committee based upon the six curricular trends outlined above. Questionnaire responses were to be narrative reports of instances in aviation education supporting one or another of the six trends outlined above.

During the Leadership Institutes of 1952 and 1953, participants volunteered further information concerning practices relevant to each of these trends, and defined a seventh significant curriculum trend receiving support from aviation education activities. This last is the trend toward extending the services of organized education to the adults of the community. Continued efforts of the AASA committee through the years of 1952 and 1953 have assembled much additional information pertaining to the study.

Following is an analysis of material gathered from cooperating school systems organized in terms of the trends which are exemplified by reported activities.

TREND NO. 1

Toward a better understanding of child growth and development, and the recognition of interest, purpose, and experience as important factors in learning

In general, it was reported that spontaneous interest in aviation may be employed to lead pupils into many different exploratory enterprises. Through it they may gain skills in locating, organizing, and evaluating information, in the exercise of critical and logical thinking, and in the practice of democratic living. Such experiences were reported as common to all maturity levels of pupils. They were planned for the maximum utilization of pupil interest and provided real and meaningful learnings whether related to areas of human living not confined to any one subject field or to classroom activities centered around the subject fields of art, music, social studies, arithmetic, reading, and science.

Detailed activities described by school systems reporting differed one from another. However, the characteristics held in common appeared to be more significant than the differences. In each instance, alert teachers capitalized on the students' natural interests, helping them to find answers to their questions and guiding them as they used the information acquired.

In Phoenix, Arizona; Los Angeles, Burbank and Fresno, California; Chicago, Illinois; Indianapolis, Indiana; Greenwood, Louisiana; Hartford City, Maryland; Duluth, Minnesota; Concord, New Hampshire; Atlantic City, New Jersey; New York, New York; Cincinnati and Columbus, Ohio—in these cities and all others reporting, the significant trends are as follows: student interests and purposes were recognized; student experiences in terms of these interests and purposes defined the classroom program. These interests, purposes, and experiences made use of aviation information which was relevant to standard curriculum areas. The following verbatim account of the program in effect at Denver, Colorado, is representative of programs reported by cooperating school systems:

We know that children learn in relation to problems and interests which have meaning for them and that behavior change is fostered or fortified through experiences in solving such problems. Examples of progressive problems in aviation which are of concern to children include the airplane itself, how it flies, what it does for people, and how it is changing economic and social relationships. Teachers therefore provide such experiences as the following to help the children to satisfy their interests and solve their problems.

Kindergarten, first, and second grades.—The children build airplanes, using boxes, boards, blocks—anything that will approximate the appearance of an airplane; they "fly" their planes, build an airport, and dramatize its activities. They go to the local airport to watch the planes on the field, the servicing of the planes, and the passengers going and coming. They create flying rhythms and sing airplane songs. They draw, paint, and construct models, and in every way are encouraged to express their interests.

Third and fourth grades.—With widening and, at the same time, more definite interests, the eight- and nine-year-olds observe, read about, and discuss the parts of an airplane, learning how each operates and why. They carry on simple experiments to build up concepts as to the characteristics of air which make flight possible. They visit the airport to explore those facilities whose purpose and operation they can understand. They, too, build airplanes and airports but with increasing attention to detail based on knowledge of the operations they are representing. They are helped to explore the work of the people who fly the planes and those who are engaged in other observable aviation jobs. Through personal experiences, newspaper articles, local events, films, and radio programs they become increasingly interested in the many uses of the airplane.

Fifth and sixth grades.—The interest in the airplane itself continues but with greater emphasis on the how and the why: safety, navigation, weather in flight, and the work of various aviation agencies. They do further experimenting and express their ideas more accurately in art, writing, and construction activities. They use maps and globes freely as they become interested in the geographic aspects of flight and as they gain new concepts of distance and direction. They are interested, above all, in the way the airplane is affecting everyday living and bringing new opportunities and problems, perhaps, to people everywhere.

All of these interests are met through such experiences as trips to the airport with definite purpose; wide reading; experimenting in the classroom "laboratory" set up in a corner of the room; interviews with "people who know," use of atlases, charts, airplane schedules, weather reports; and "flight experience" in the Link demonstrator.   Subject field?   We do not worry too much about the specific subject area in which the child is working in his aviation experiences.   In satisfying his interests and solving his problems, the child makes use of, in purposeful situations, all possible subject areas.   He needs to read; to prove scientific facts; to locate places and trace routes on maps and globes; to exchange ideas with others; to handle numbers as the airplane problem under discussion demands them; to write letters, stories, and reports; and to express his ideas in many creative ways.   This learning proceeds most effectively because it has meaning and purpose to the child.

Junior high school.—Here the interests in aviation are more often integrated with social studies, science, English, and art, but the problem approach is used and further experiences such as those described in the preceding section are provided.

Senior high school.—More definite channeling of the interests of young people in aviation occurs at this level.   Some of them become interested in preaeronautics classes.   The vocational aspects of flight attract many.   Most important, however, is the interest in the airplane in relation to international understandings.   Courses in relation to these interests are provided.

TREND No. 2

Toward the recognition of the school's responsibility to help students understand the complex age in which they live, and through guided experience to help them to assume responsibility for the improvement of life

A curriculum which is responsive to the challenges of present-day living must seek to develop aviation understandings in order that students may acquire the necessary skills for effective democratic citizenship.   Aviation is an important and relatively new factor in modern living which finds expression through the social, political, economic, and spiritual problems of our times.   For this reason, aviation content, materials, and experiences should be woven into many curriculum areas.

Typical of the basic air-age understandings to be considered in curriculum planning is the following classification recognized by the schools of Indiana:

1. Sociological concepts—The interaction of cultures in a shrinking world; the influence of aviation on the communication of ideas; the effects of aviation on individual, group, and state thinking; and the changes in patterns of living induced by air transportation.

2. Geographical concepts—The geographical location of major air routes and airports throughout the world; the relationship between strategic locations and air power; the determination of distance in terms of time; the values of air transportation to the consumer; and the influence of aviation on the industrial development of hitherto inaccessible areas.

3. Political and economic concepts—Governmental agencies and boards which regulate aviation; importance of aviation in the quest for world peace; effects of air power on national security; history of federal aid to aviation; influence of aviation on the local community; the place of the aviation industry in our national economy; and vocational opportunities in aviation.

The Minneapolis, Minnesota, schools formulated four basic principles of air-age citizenship: (1) A recognition of the responsibility for an equitable sharing of the world's human and natural resources. (2) A genuine acceptance of the essential neighborliness produced by the new concepts of time and space. (3) An appreciation of the varying cultures of the world and of the problems encountered in making maximum use of these cultural resources. (4) An understanding of the way in which the airplane can either prevent or achieve an effective world citizenship.

Cincinnati, Ohio, schools related aviation education to understanding aviation's impacts upon world cultures, in the following terms: (1) Diminishing differences among the cultures of the world as a result of air transportation. (2) Increased understanding among the peoples of the world as a result of air transportation. (3) Increased international trade as a result of the air age. (4) Greater need for natural resources upon which aviation is dependent. (5) Changes in the total cultural life of the world as a result of the air age.

Children are helped to develop the above concepts. Emphasis is placed upon use of the materials of aviation at all maturity levels. A first-grade unit, for example, might take on new interest in airplanes because the father of one of the children does much of his traveling by air. Fifth-graders, in learning the history of their country, might gain a concept of a shrinking world through a study of time taken for travel by air between different locations. A twelfth-grade physics class might draw its illustrations of principles from aerodynamics.

Emphasis at all levels is placed upon the development of the following attitudes important to aviation.

1. *The necessity for an understanding of the various cultures of the world.* Even though primary children are concerned chiefly with family living and the immediate community, in many schools there are increasing numbers of children of displaced persons bringing new cultural patterns. Many fathers or relatives of primary children flew planes in World War II and discussed with these boys and girls how quickly France, Japan, and other countries can be reached. They brought back pictures, souvenirs, and stories of the people of foreign countries, so that the horizon of primary children has been expanding. Many misconceptions of other peoples are being replaced with actual firsthand accounts of their patterns of living.

Many children have traveled by plane to visit relatives

and so are very conscious of time in relation to distance. They are continually asking how long would it take by plane, by train, by car?

2. *The maximum use of these cultures for the common good.* Studies have shown that prejudice and intolerance are learned. Boys and girls are more inclined to be curious about and interested in other children who, because of language handicap or mannerism, are different from them. They are eager to learn new games and new songs and to hear about places which are different. They are quick to accept or reject new ways of doing things.

Since air travel has virtually removed the barriers of distance between countries, it is important that children be helped to evaluate the good cultural patterns from all countries and in turn ask for evaluation of their patterns by children of other cultures. It is important also that children be helped to see the vital role geographical location plays in determining not only the basic needs of people—food, clothes, shelter—but also the development of large cities, air routes, and air bases.

3. *Individual and group responsibility for the achievement of world citizenship.* Everyday classroom living which provides opportunity for developing leadership and group planning, is building solidly the foundations for world citizenship. If the individual does not have respect for himself and cannot see the need for his contribution in the total design, he cannot help others or be helped to develop a program in which all may work together peacefully.

Without exception, all cooperating schools recognized aviation as a factor in the complexities of the time and reported giving classroom attention to the problems of modern life which aviation has generated. The students were guided to appropriate understandings through experiences centered around such problems. The examples of reports cited above are typical only in terms of objectives. Details of activities were defined by the talents and degree of creative imagination of individuals involved in classroom programs.

Trend No. 3

Toward a growing realization of the school's responsibility to education for vocational competence and to help youth choose a career

The programs provided for students interested in aviation careers may be placed in two categories, (*a*) nonvocational, and (*b*) vocational. The nonvocational group usually includes such preflight courses as are offered in Columbus, Dallas, Denver, Los Angeles, Philadelphia, and Syracuse. Toledo offers an aircraft engine tryout course, and Portland provides aircraft, engine, and ground instruction. Other cities like Washington, D. C., and Omaha include an aviation interest course or survey course which provides general background in the field. The industrial arts program in many cities includes model airplane construction, aircraft drafting, aerodynamics, Link Trainer, navigation, and meteorology. In Chicago, Detroit, and Indianapolis, to mention a few systems, guidance information includes the study of job requirements for aviation occupations. The program of the Civil Air Patrol is gaining increasing acceptance as a credit course in the high school curriculum of many cities.

Special courses are offered in trade and vocational programs throughout the country for students desiring technical training in aviation. In general, these courses are designed to qualify students for employment in the field following the completion of training in engine and aircraft work. These programs in a number of cities are certificated by the Civil Aeronautics Administration. In other cases such approval is contemplated. The following cities reported that they are now offering courses which are fully or partially approved by the Civil Aeronautics Administration: Akron, Boston, Cincinnati, Chicago, Detroit, Minneapolis, New York City, and Pittsburgh. A notable example of a highly organized vocational program in aeronautics is the Manhattan Trade School in New York City.

A good example of reports of aviation education supporting Trend No. 3 is that of Paul F. Devine, director of Instructional Aids and Services Branch of the Los Angeles, California, school system.

During the school year 1952–53 the Aviation Education Flight Program at Garfield High School and Franklin High School was continued with some changes. Because of closing of the East Los Angeles Airport, the flight program was transferred to the Glendale Airport. The arrangements for transporting pupils to and from the airport were materially improved.

Agreements were reached between Mr. Reeves, assistant superintendent, Mr. Holt, principal of Franklin High School, and Mr. Brothers, principal of Garfield High School, regarding the furnishing of transportation by the Board of Education for the purposes of the program. This assures that each pupil will be properly covered by school insurance throughout the entire program. Also, the teachers will no longer be required to furnish transportation to pupils without expense to the school system.

This classroom is specifically adapted to the flight instructional program and it is now used by our pupils according to schedule. While one group is receiving flight instruction in the air, the other group receives ground school instruction in the classroom. Both instructors, Mr. Kindy and Mr. Tower, are well pleased with this new arrangement.

At Westchester High School, Mr. Heusdens carries on specific aviation instruction as a definite part of his course in physical science. For the values to be gained in motivation, educational background, and vocational guidance, Mr. Heusdens' classes undertook trips to the International Airport and the California Aero School of Aeronautics. Both of these trips are listed in

"It's Worth a Visit" (our handbook on field trips). In planning for the visits, specific instruction was given to the pupils relating to the learnings and observations to be anticipated. Also, a follow-up in the form of questions and notebook assignments, was given as part of the assignment.

At Narbonne High School, Mr. Stembridge carried on a program in physical science with emphasis on aviation, weather-map reading, aeronautical charts, and the air age in general. A trip to the Long Beach Airport was a part of the integrated work. Because Mr. Stembridge was beginning this type of work he was provided with an opportunity to visit Mr. Kindy at Franklin High School for the purpose of becoming better acquainted with the possibilities for air-age education. He was supplied with aeronautical section charts, meteorological charts, daily weather maps in diurnal sequence, as well as other supplementary material.

At Washington High School, Mr. Morey Miller carried on a well-established air-age education program in which the classroom is set up as both a laboratory and a library center for resource material in the field. It is equipped with a Link Trainer, power plant, charts, navigational charts, and so forth. This laboratory-library is a resource center for the entire school as well as for classes in physical science.

Throughout the city physics and physical science teachers give specific instruction in physical principles, which are applied in air science—such as Bernoulli effect, venturi tubes, lift, weight, drag, friction, air pressure, meteorology, instrument structure, instrument reading, instrument calibrations, the laws of gravitation, and the laws of motion. The new texts in mathematics give more problems than before which are related to aviation, the air age, fuel consumption, estimated time of arrival, rate, time, distance, navigation, and so forth.

At the present writing, the aviation industry is classed as the second largest industry in the United States. Los Angeles is the capital city for this industry and maintains a $15,000,000 per week payroll within the metropolitan area. This places a definite responsibility upon the schools of Los Angeles City with respect to aviation curriculum and education in our schools. We feel that we are meeting this responsibility.

TREND NO. 4

Toward a more integrated organization of the curriculum, and the use of the large center of interest as a frame of reference

In those schools where the curriculum is organized around broad human problems, such as Living and Working Together, or Intercultural Understanding, special emphasis is given to the part which aviation plays.

The Indiana State Department of Education suggests introducing aviation materials into six areas as integral parts of units of study: Living and Working Together, Discovering Our World of Science, Improving Our Physical Well-Being, Thinking and Working With Numbers, Communicating Ideas, and Expressing Ourselves Creatively. Within the first-named area, Living and Working Together, aviation concepts are allocated in the various levels as follows:

Primary	Intermediate	Upper
Understanding in a simple way what air transportation is	Understanding modern air transportation	Understanding modern air transportation
Comparing air transportation with other kinds	Understanding the development of air transportation and what its future is	Learning how aviation affects the lives of people
Learning about aviation helpers	Learning how the airplane is making the people of the world more interdependent	Understanding the part played by aviation in the world's interdependence
Finding out ways in which we depend upon aviation	Understanding the government regulations that are essential in the air age	Understanding the government regulations that are essential in the air age

In the Kansas City Social Studies Unit Program, the units on transportation and communication include sections on aviation. In grade 5, for example, the unit includes the topic "Explorers of the Air."

In Oakland, California, the impact of aviation on democracy is considered in a course entitled "Problems in Democracy."

In Atlanta, Georgia, the role of aviation in industry in the future development of the city is included in eighth-grade citizenship classes.

In Dallas, Texas, a unit treating the value of the airplane in our daily lives is included in a ninth-grade social studies course.

In Columbus, Ohio, the curriculum of the schools at present consists of broad subject fields. The centers of interest around which learning experiences are organized fall within these subject fields. The description of curricular experiences indicates, however, that the units which evolved in a subject field such as English or social studies soon cut across several other fields. For example, if one examines the wide range and variety of learning activities engaged in by pupils as they explored the unit on "Our Shrinking World" and its implications for aviation education, he will see that these experiences cannot be categorized as any one subject. They involve language arts, art, and music, as well as basic social understandings.

Consequently, although the curricular structure is subject-centered, whenever a large unit of work is undertaken it soon draws on many other related fields.

Winfield, Kansas, reports that not only are there units of aviation, but also in most of the units in science, mathematics, and social science, aviation education materials are used to add interest, information, and to further the general understanding.

Hartford, Connecticut, makes the following statement:

Science.—There are many areas of science in which aviation can be related. It comes in the study of weather, air, instruments, navigation, etc. At the intermediate and upper grade levels we find considerable material relating to airplanes and aviation in the regular and supplementary books on science.

Social Studies.—Communication and transportation are two areas or units which are found at almost every level in our elementary schools. The effects of the improved facilities in these areas are closely related to aviation. Also, the study of maps and globes is related to air routes and similar phases of aviation.

Arithmetic.—Comparative costs of travel by various types of transportation facilities, computing mileages, reading timetables, etc., are found at every grade level in many of our schools.

Health and Safety.—In both of these areas the impact of aviation can be found. Such things as the effect of high altitudes and speed on the human body, precautionary measures around airplanes and airports, preventative measures for greater safety in air travel, etc.

A seventh-grade unit reported by New York City was entitled "Adjusting Ourselves to the Air Age." Four areas of the curriculum were integrated in the study of this unit. These were language arts, social studies, mathematics, science.

This unit was teacher-pupil planned; it evolved because of the importance of aviation in our modern world. Students learned that aviation plays an important part in our lives and helps bring closer harmony to the people of the world. Some of the experiences which grew out of this unit are listed below:

1. Observing motion pictures and slides
2. Discussing current events of air-age significance
3. Participating in class planning
4. Taking trips to museums, airports, airline exhibits, aircraft factories, weather bureau
5. Personally participating in air experience activities: (*a*) airplane controls; (*b*) boarding a plane; (*c*) Link Trainer manipulation
6. Attending talks by Air Force personnel
7. Listening to talks by air education officials

8. Collecting free and inexpensive materials
9. Organizing and caring for classroom library and laboratory of air-age material
10. Building miniature models of airplanes.
11. Conducting experiments concerned with air-flight science
12. Handling aircraft instruments
13. Recording and evaluating weather data
14. Using globes and maps
15. Obtaining air-age information through correspondence

In common with the schools cited above, all reporting schools gave examples of the employment of relevant aviation information in the building of units of study, supplementing subject-matter areas, or enriching classroom programs defined by student needs and interests.

Trend No. 5

Toward a wider use of community and school resources as aids to learning: for example, the field trip and participation in neighborhood projects

Most of the returns from school systems show that the community is becoming a veritable laboratory for meaningful experiences with aviation. Major resources in the community which are used extensively to enrich and vitalize learnings are included in the following list of illustrations: (1) Firsthand observations of airport facilities such as hangars, airplanes, ticket offices, control tower, weather bureau, commissary, etc.; (2) Visits to airline companies and manufacturing plants; (3) Student conferences with aviation personnel; (4) Visitations in aeronautics classes in vocational and trade schools, colleges, and universities; (5) Contacts with local, state, and national aviation agencies and organizations such as state departments of aeronautics, Civil Aeronautics Administration, Civil Air Patrol, Air National Guard, Wing Scouts, the Air Foundation, Flying Farmers, airport commissions, and many others.

Additional resources utilized in several communities include: government air bases, the Link Trainer, private flying schools, research laboratories of government and industry, air demonstration centers, mobile air centers, and national air races.

Almost without exception, school systems have commented on the use of various supplementary materials to develop air-age understandings. These include:

1. Radio and television programs
2. Films
3. Slides
4. Models
5. Charts
6. Maps
7. Globes
8. Pamphlets
9. Magazines
10. Newspapers

The survey demonstrates that this trend is being readily accepted by most communities as a definite part of a well-balanced school curriculum.

Reports revealed that in New York City school children take many trips for pleasure, investigation, discovery, and study. The education of children in the schools of New York is closely linked with their living in the community. The school has a responsibility for expanding the classroom to include the resources of the community in which the child lives. In most cases, unless children are taken by their teachers to see the actual operation of industry, government, and social organizations, many of them have little opportunity to obtain any firsthand information about the work of the world. Children's efforts to solve their problems are aided greatly by excursions, interviewing people, and by other varied activities which are primary sources of research.

The Board of Transportation of the City of New York grants free transportation to New York City school children to make excursions possible.

Phoenix, Arizona, reports that the schools have had excellent help from the Municipal Airport as well as the Phoenix College Flying School. Trips have included opportunities to go through a Constellation, the control tower, communications and weather bureaus, the ticket office and waiting rooms at the Municipal Airport; the children have had opportunities to see and "fly" in the Link Trainer, hear explanations and see demonstrations of the workings of a model airplane, and explore the hangars.

Transportation in a school bus is secured by the teacher calling the Municipal Administration Building and requesting the bus. The number of trips is limited by the fact that two buses must serve a large number of classes in twenty-two schools. The teacher is requested to take the trip before she arranges to go with her class, and she is required to have permission slips signed by the parents.

In Richmond, Virginia, wide and consistent use is made by the schools of the aviation resources available. A field trip to the Byrd Airport is probably the most popular trip, next to a historical tour of the city, that the school children of Richmond experience.

TREND NO. 6

Toward the acceptance of in-service education as a permanent need of the schools and as an integral aspect of curriculum improvement

A great number of school systems are providing programs of teacher education through which goals for aviation education are defined and materials identified. Teacher education projects are found at the local, state, and national levels. Brief descriptions of some of the in-service courses reported by participants in the current study follow.

During the school year of 1946–47 Baltimore initiated a series of one-day aviation institutes at the municipal airport which included: observation of weather bureau operations, air traffic control; a conducted flight over the city; and lectures from leading authorities. Recommendations were drafted for desirable emphasis on aviation in various subject-matter areas.

Monthly workshops held in Washington, D.C., utilized children's questions as the basis of study with the science department, providing suggestions as to materials and methods for dealing with these interests in an academic manner.

In Philadelphia, one course in aviation education per year has been included in the in-service education program since 1946. General background is supplied through field trips, demonstrations, round-table discussions on curriculum resources. Chartered flights on commercial airlines to a foreign port were a special feature of the 1948 course.

Denver's on-going program in air-age education includes: a three-day conference in 1946, summer workshops for the past three years, cooperation with the University of Denver in the use of a Link Trainer, a classroom demonstration project involving several teachers.

From Cincinnati, Dallas, Oakland, and San Francisco, special representatives have been sent to various demonstration centers. In Kansas City three institutes have been held. Actual flight experience has been offered teachers in Los Angeles and New Orleans. In Minneapolis, flights were offered to all central office staff members and to all principals in the school system. The in-service course for teachers provided for airport tours and flight experience as well as the general academic background of aviation. During 1948 more than one thousand elementary and secondary teachers in Chicago were provided firsthand experience at the municipal airport.

In some cities, San Diego among them, mobile units and air centers have been organized to give teachers the necessary know-how in regard to aviation education. In laboratory settings, teachers may examine books, charts, pamphlets, films and recordings; observe classroom teaching, and in some instances "fly" in a Link Trainer.

Indications are that there is a growing tendency for in-service teacher education to accommodate aviation interest.

TREND NO. 7

Toward extending the services of organized education to the adults of the community

Reports from school systems represented at the Washington Aviation Education Leadership Institutes outline four types of extension service significant in terms of aviation education.

Those systems having adequate facilities offer to adults both day school and evening classes in such subjects as air navigation, meteorology, aircraft engines, and aircraft. Among such systems are Buffalo, New York City, Los Angeles, and Chicago. Other school systems report courses in aviation for farmers. The State Department of Education in South Carolina reports such courses in certain of South Carolina's schools. Seminars and air travel courses are reported as extension offerings of the schools of California.

In other school systems parents of children in school and other adults of the community participate in airport operations institutes. Pontiac, Michigan, reports attendance at such institutes to number as many as six hundred adults.

A third type of adult education program recruits representative citizens for service on aviation education committees. Standing committees composed of laymen and schoolmen usually gain both the objectives for which organized and also succeed as an instructional device. Much about aviation can be learned through the interchange of information which takes place when committees are at work.

Tulsa, Oklahoma; St. Cloud, Minnesota; and Burbank, California; report a fourth type of extension service. In these and other cities whose extension service is similar, out-of-school groups pursuing educational objectives in aviation are provided with instructional aids, such as reference books and motion picture films.

7. Summary and Conclusions

THIS REPORT PRESENTS experiences which indicate that air-age education is essentially a part of many phases of instruction in our schools and enters naturally and helpfully into the curriculum on both elementary and secondary levels. It shows, further, that aviation content and materials serve to enrich and vitalize learning when fused into subject fields in the existing curriculum framework and/or when considered as a separate area of experiencing. While many promising school practices are currently in evidence throughout the country, it must be recognized that a rapidly changing social scene and the crucial problems emerging require continual adjustments in the educational program. It was with the hope of sharpening the possibilities of mutual cooperation between two great areas, education and aviation, that this study was undertaken.

ANALYSIS OF THE AVIATION QUESTIONNAIRE

Responses were received from 100 cooperating school systems: 87 local systems, 12 state systems, and the Territory of Alaska. It is significant that in Alaska, where aviation is a vital necessity because of the distances between settled areas, aviation education was most constructive and concrete.

Data were requested on each trend (as specified in chapter vi), but there was a tendency on the part of the answers to overlap, and it is recognized that school procedures for integrating aviation content into subject-matter courses employ some of the same techniques and devices for any age and maturity level. For example, on all levels except possibly kindergarten and the first two or three grades of elementary school, field trips to airports, aircraft plants, and factories producing aviation parts, and to schools offering aviation training, and classroom visits by resource people (pilots, stewardesses, mechanics, and others, including representatives of government agencies), these provide most effective teaching to supplement books, pamphlets, charts, maps, models, films, and other visual aids.

Trend 1, aviation as a factor in child growth and development, was reflected in such statements as: "Any work or activity involving the airplane immediately appeals to any group," "Aviation is of interest at all stages of development and growth."

Many schools expressed the thought quoted above. The degree of interest shown and the application of that interest to the student's personal problems ranges all the way from sheer entertainment, say, in the kindergarten to practical considerations in choosing a career in high school. Implicit in the program in the higher elementary grades and in secondary school is the building of better citizenship through knowledge and understanding of other lands and other peoples—knowledge to which aviation has contributed mightily by "shrinking" world distances and making possible more interchange of visitors between countries.

The tendency to integrate aviation throughout the entire educational system, stressing various activities or subjects, at different age or grade levels, is illustrated by the following outline embodying reports from various schools:

Kindergarten, grades 1–2: Toys, stories, games, pictures, paper planes, description of pilot's work, etc.

Grades 3–4: Study of transportation and communication, and geography in relation to social studies, especially the manners, mores, and customs of different peoples.

Grades 5–6: Study of science, involving drawings, model construction, and scientific principles of transportation.

Grades 7–8: Geography and arithmetic, involving a computation of time and distance schedules.

Grades 7–12: Industrial arts, general science, physics, and mathematics mostly stressed aviation material, but history, English, and the language arts were also mentioned several times.

Grades 9–12: Special courses in meteorology, mechanical drawing, map making, aerodynamics, aircraft mechanics; and special activities such as art projects, clubs, Air or Wing Scouts, Civil Air Patrol, etc., were included in the responses.

Activities demonstrating Trends 2 and 4 overlap since "recognition of the school's responsibility to help students understand the complex age in which they live, and through guided experience to help them to assume responsibility for the improvement of life" necessarily involves "a more integrated organization of the curriculum." That these objectives are greatly aided by aviation was a practically unanimous conclusion of the responding schools. The schools' experiences in integrating aviation content and materials into subject-matter courses are summarized as follows:

Social studies (civics, history, economics, and geography): The study of transportation, communication, mobility of population; elimination of prejudice and development of tolerance; social, political, and economic factors of the world-community. Use of field trips and all visual aids, especially air-age and global maps.

Science: Study of air, weather, principles of flight. Experiments around problems in the field of aeronautics; making model planes, weather maps. Emphasis by teacher on the open-minded scientific approach, cooperation, and individual responsibility.

Mathematics: Problems in relative speeds and distances, load capacity, scale models, graphs, etc.

Health and safety: Study of physiological aspects of flight.

English and language arts: Readings—especially in areas which show the social and economic influence of aviation on people throughout the world; dramatizations, compositions; historical aspects through library references, current developments reported in periodicals.

Art: Posters, pictures, designs of models, airports, etc.

Special courses: Industrial arts, mechanics, geology, aerodynamics, meteorology, theory of flight, logistics, etc.

Trend 3, the growing realization of the school's responsibility for vocational competence and for helping young people to choose a career, is evidenced by the overwhelming majority of responses indicating the use of the guidance department in counseling. Many secondary schools hold Career Days, stressing specific job opportunities and occupations. Planned programs designed to give specific vocational help to the students include: (*a*) field trips to airports, factories, and schools offering aviation training; (*b*) resource people from aviation agencies or industries, speeches at assemblies, and educational or vocational conferences; (*c*) special aviation courses in the schools (aerodynamics, meteorology, airplane mechanics, theory of flight, etc.); (*d*) use of art classes to prepare posters.

If a career is worth while, there is social responsibility connected with it. The progress of industry depends upon the personnel's ability to assume responsibility; in aviation, people's lives depend upon this. People have confidence to the extent that carriers prove safe and dependable—both machinery and men. The importance of a youth's choice of a life-career as a social contribution is stressed throughout the curriculum. Some of the devices used by schools to this end were: (1) Opportunities provided in the community for exploration of interests, sharing social relationships and responsibility through leadership and service, and stressing character development; (2) Use of resource people (pilots, stewardesses, mechanics, etc.); (3) Use of homeroom and social studies discussions on vocational subjects. (4) Special activities—dramatizations; visits to airports to study duties and responsibilities of personnel, flight schedules, etc.; and vocational courses stressing expertness and precision.

Trend 5, the wider use of community resources as aids to

learning about aviation and the many areas connected with it, was reported almost universally. Virtually all schools accessible to airports and aviation facilities and industries make trips to airports, factories, exhibits, museums, and weather stations. A few schools reported such trips as "rare," many schools reported "several" during each school year, some reported "frequent." In arranging such trips, the following steps are suggested as helpful: (1) Permission from parents for airport visitation is practically always required, and for the most part easily obtained; (2) Substitute teachers or parents help in supervision; in one case reported the school nurse helped; (3) Other teachers cooperate by taking charge of nonparticipants; or in some cases, principals or supervisors supervise them; (4) Principals prepare rules of conduct, check supervision of participants, provide for non-participants, adjust staff schedules, etc.; (5) In some cases, field trips are conducted after school hours or in weekend time; (6) An almost equal number of schools use school buses, chartered commercial vehicles, or private cars.

Teachers prepare carefully for such trips so that the children will have adequate background for understanding what they see and be able to ask intelligent questions. Procedures reported include: (1) Questions formulated by teacher and students jointly in discussions in advance of trip; (2) Visual aids (pictures, diagrams, charts, graphs, filmstrips, films, slides, etc.) are usually available; (3) In many cases model airplanes are built; (4) In one case the local Civil Aeronautics Administration educationist was used; (5) In eleven cases arrangements for flights by students were provided on the field trip, with parents' permission; (6) In five cases CAA courses (meteorology, navigation, mechanics, aerial photography, radio telephone, aircraft, etc.) were provided; (7) In five cases Civil Air Patrol courses of a similar nature were provided; (8) Library materials were used; also newspaper and magazine articles; (9) In a number of cases airlines literature was utilized in advance of trips, or military flying charts were studied; (10) In several cases a model weather station was operated.

Trend 6, toward the acceptance of in-service training of teachers as an integral aspect of curriculum development, was widely accepted in theory, but generally no specific opportunities were made available to teachers in the schools reporting.

However, in twenty cases, state or local workshops were held, and in-service air education classes and university science courses were offered. In several cases, courses arranged by CAA were available. In one case a special aviation course was offered on a scholarship basis. Trips to airports and factories, air shows, and exhibits were made in eight cases, and in ten instances flights over local areas were made available for teachers. In three cases, teacher conferences on integration of aviation throughout the curriculum were reported.

Summary of Questionnaire Reports

1. Most school systems that responded to the questionnaire did not mention specific age, grade, subject classifications of material, nor did they send photographs or supplementary material.

2. In almost 50 percent of the cases reported, little or no provision is being made for aviation education. However, the questionnaire has made it evident that there is a great range of diversity in this respect. The range is from absolutely nothing and an evident lack of interest to a very high interest and a well-organized, integrated, and special curriculum in the field of aviation education. This would be an expected result in view of the difference in needs of various localities, and differing stages of educational development and opportunity in our forty-eight school systems.

3. Civil Aeronautics Administration and Civil Air Patrol

courses of study and assistance are being utilized to some extent, but schools could profit by a much greater use of these facilities.

4. Airlines literature and visitations of their personnel to the schools are an important stimulus to inclusion of aviation material in the curriculum. When airports are in close enough proximity to the schools to offer class visitation, additional stimulus to aviation is provided.

5. There is evidence that integration of aviation materials is being practiced successfully in several areas of the curriculum, especially in social studies, science, and mathematics.

CONCLUSIONS BASED UPON REPORTS FROM SCHOOL SYSTEMS

The analysis and conclusions reported above depended in great part upon responses from contributing school systems received in 1951. Information from these school systems subsequently received and analyzed reveals that in many instances the 1953 aviation education situation has changed little from that of 1951.

It is of significance to note that the aviation education movement has gained rapid acceleration during the years 1952 and 1953 in the fifty school systems and communities represented by staff-level personnel at the Leadership Institutes, as shown by the following tabulation:

	Yes (%)	No (%)
Aviation education is among the school system's offerings	100	
Aviation education activities are employed in the elementary school	85	4½
Aviation education activities are employed in the secondary school	93	
Aviation information is used to supplement course offerings when relevant	93	
An aviation course or aviation courses are offered	64	28
Aviation courses are offered in the vocational or technical high school or in the junior college	40	8½
Our community has an aviation education committee	41	34
We contemplate organizing an aviation education committee	40	11

The general problem areas in aviation education relate to educational policy, to teacher education in appropriate techniques and content, and to the preparation of adequate and appropriate instructional materials.

The studies reported offer evidence that in terms of accelerating the aviation education movement, an important step is to stimulate the attention and enlist the interest of school administrators. In this regard, it is well not to overlook the cooperative help forthcoming from the school patrons.

It may be concluded from the information revealed through the efforts of those contributing to this project, that aviation education is only one aspect of a much more comprehensive educational movement, that its problems are problems common to education generally. Aviation enters the picture not only because it can be translated into military power, and is thus a major factor in our national destiny and perhaps in the survival of Western civilization, but also because its impact upon all fields of peaceful pursuits make it as powerful as, if not more powerful than, that of any other contemporary social force.